The Practice of
Authentic
PLCs

A Guide to
Effective
Teacher
Teams

Daniel R. Venables

CORWIN
A SAGE Company

For information:

Corwin
A SAGE Company
2455 Teller Road
Thousand Oaks, California 91320
(800) 233-9936
Fax: (800) 417-2466
www.corwin.com

SAGE Ltd.
1 Oliver's Yard
55 City Road
London EC1Y 1SP
United Kingdom

SAGE India Pvt. Ltd.
B 1/I 1 Mohan Cooperative
    Industrial Area
Mathura Road, New Delhi 110 044
India

SAGE Asia-Pacific Pte. Ltd.
33 Pekin Street #02-01
Far East Square
Singapore 048763

Printed in the United States of America

Library of Congress Cataloging-in-Publication Data

Venables, Daniel R.
The practice of authentic PLCs: a guide to effective teacher teams/Daniel R. Venables.
    p. cm.
Includes bibliographical references and index.
ISBN 978-1-4129-8663-2 (pbk.)
  1. Professional learning communities. 2. Teaching teams. I. Title.

LB1731.V39 2011
371.14'8—dc22   2010044643

This book is printed on acid-free paper.

11 12 13 14 15 10 9 8 7 6 5 4 3 2 1

Acquisitions Editor:	Debra Stollenwerk
Associate Editor:	Desirée A. Bartlett
Editorial Assistant:	Kimberly Greenberg
Production Editor:	Cassandra Margaret Seibel
Copy Editor:	Tina Hardy
Typesetter:	C&M Digitals (P) Ltd.
Proofreader:	Jenifer Kooiman
Indexer:	Jean Casalegno
Cover Designer:	Karine Hovsepian
Permissions Editor:	Adele Hutchinson

Contents

Preface

That Professional Learning Communities (PLCs) have become the talk of educators these days is curious to me, for two reasons. The first is that it has taken painfully long for educators to realize that working in isolation is inherently limited in its ability to help us improve. We get it now: collectively, we *are* more than the sum of our parts. The second reason for my curiosity rests in the fact that PLCs have, in small pockets of education, been around for nearly two decades. PLCs were called Critical Friends Groups (CFGs) back in the early 1990s and I was fortunate to have been trained and fully immersed in this work beginning in 1993. During that year, I began an intensive two-year training program as a Math/Science Fellow for the Coalition of Essential Schools (CES), based then at Brown University in Providence, Rhode Island. At the conclusion of this program in 1994, I became a member of the National Re:Learning Faculty of CES (renamed and reconfigured as the National School Reform Faculty, or NSRF, in 1995). To this day, the NSRF (based now at the Harmony Education Center in Bloomington, Indiana), along with a splinter group called the School Reform Initiative (also based in Bloomington), continue to provide some of the very best resources for working PLCs.

Several schools and many CFGs/PLCs later, I began to see the work of CES and NSRF multiply and take hold in many larger pockets of education. As this happened, I began to witness a change in culture in many schools and districts. These changes impacted the way teachers worked. Common planning time for teacher teams became widespread; collaboration became valued and practiced in urban and rural schools alike. As team planning and collaboration became more commonplace in lieu of the teacher-in-isolation model that lingered for nearly a century, the term Professional Learning Community (or more commonly, PLC) entered into our educational vernacular. As has been the case with so many terms and acronyms that abbreviate various educational reform efforts, the term PLC became ubiquitous and, by virtue of that very fact, its meaning and focus became diluted and often obscured. Suddenly every group of teachers at every kind of teacher meeting was labeled a *PLC*. To be fair and honest to those teams of teachers working as authentic PLCs, many groups deserved the title, but many others did not. Assembling a group of teachers during common planning time is in and of itself no more a PLC than putting kids in groups is a cooperative learning environment. That would be disappointing enough, but the danger in calling any group of teachers a PLC is that everyone in the school community thinks they are in and understand genuine PLCs. When no real gain in student learning resulted from such groups, the teachers' and administrators' mentality resounded: "Yeah, we're doing[1] PLCs," or worse, "PLCs are nothing new—we've been doing them for years." And so the tacit belief in many schools became that PLCs don't really work. The problem was not that PLCs didn't work; the problem was that what many schools were calling PLCs didn't work.

I wrote this book to help real schools build authentic PLCs with real faculties. There are several important works on PLCs written by distinguished authors who present convincing research-based arguments for why schools should have PLCs. *The Practice of Authentic PLCs* does not attempt to convince readers to implement PLCs, and it is not about the research supporting PLCs (though a brief research summary is included in Chapter 1). This book is about how to actually build, from the ground up, effective, authentic PLCs in any school or district.

The Practice of Authentic PLCs is not a step-by-step PLC owner's manual. Nothing as complex as building genuine, collaborative teacher cultures focused entirely on student learning could ever be expressed completely in a book that would work for every teacher team in every school. There is no cookie-cutter approach to this work that could accommodate every school faculty. But there are some common truths that are characteristic of authentic PLCs that are worth discussing. *The Practice of Authentic PLCs* acts as a guide for teachers, teacher leaders, and administrators in assisting schools in creating and using authentic PLCS, so that student learning really does improve quantitatively and qualitatively.

The Practice of Authentic PLCs is organized into three parts. Part I (Chapters 1 and 2) provides background and clarity about PLCs and lays the foundation for building a collaborative culture in a school.

Chapter 1 delineates PLCs and provides a research base explaining the essential impact of PLCs on improving student achievement.

Chapter 2 lays out the progression of steps that are vital to building effective, collaborative teacher teams. Team building, norm setting, and first exposure to using protocols are essential elements in this chapter. Everything that follows Chapter 2 depends on teacher teams having a solid foundation of collaboration with which to do the work of authentic PLCs.

Part II (Chapters 3, 4, and 5) provides the foreground, which is the work, or *Essential Tasks*, of authentic PLCs. Respectively, Chapters 3, 4, and 5 explain how to examine teacher and student work, design quality

---

1. This statement is inherently oxymoronic. As those who are involved with authentic PLCs will attest, PLCs are not so much something the team *does*, as they are something that the team *is*.

common formative assessments, and review and respond to data. These chapters walk the reader through each of these Essential Tasks in which authentic PLCs continually engage.

The final two chapters, 6 and 7, comprise Part III: Coaching Authentic PLCs. This section assists the coaches of PLCs, those teacher leaders who facilitate the complex and interpersonal tasks outlined in the previous chapters. This aspect of authentic PLCs—guidance for the PLC coaches—is too often neglected in popular works in the PLC realm and, in my view, is absolutely essential if PLCs are to make a difference for the students whose teachers are part of a PLC.

Chapter 6 offers coaches practical guidance in facilitating the protocols and activities mentioned throughout Parts I and II and ends with a Frequently Asked Questions section that addresses questions I am commonly asked by coaches in working with schools. A more detailed discussion of troubleshooting more substantial obstacles faced by coaches is the subject of the final Chapter 7.

Part III concludes with a Coach's Appendix, which provides important reference documents that coaches can use to gauge their teams' progress as they lead their PLCs toward authenticity. These documents include the following: *PLC Members' Code of Discourse, High Functioning PLC Continuum,* and *Suggested First-Year Timeline.* In addition to the Coach's Appendix, there is a section following Part III that includes all protocols and activities mentioned throughout the text, as well as some new protocols for team building, looking at student and teacher work, problem solving issues and dilemmas, engaging in text-based discussions, and looking at data.

Everything suggested in this book has been field-tested in schools where I have taught or in schools in which I have consulted in the ways of implementing PLCs. So while the content of this book is supported by research, the book is not based solely on the research. It is based on my firsthand experiences working in and with PLCs for almost 20 years. Its genesis derives not so much from wanting to write a handbook about how to build authentic PLCs, but from a need I recognized while working with school districts.

On a final note, it is important to realize that building authentic PLCs is not a linear task. That is, with the exception of team building and setting group norms, which should be done at the outset, many of the Essential Tasks of PLCs described in Part II (e.g., looking at student work, designing common formative assessments, responding to data) can be tackled in any order, and indeed, they should happen concurrently in a PLC. There is no one way to do this; it will be a recurring theme of this book that PLCs are not so much a checklist of tasks as they are a culture within a school, a culture whose players are committed to quality and collaborative teacher work that focuses without compromise or exception on improving student learning.

Daniel R. Venables
Cornelius, North Carolina
June 2010

Acknowledgments

I would be remiss in a work like this if I did not acknowledge the contributions of Rick and Becky DuFour and Bob Eaker for making PLCs a "schoolhousehold" word. Their work has convinced American educators that PLCs are a good idea and it has paved the way for me to write about how to actually implement PLCs and do so authentically. Other significant authors whose works have influenced my thinking include Doug Reeves, Mike Schmoker, Grant Wiggins, Larry Ainsworth, Mike Mattos, Bob Marzano, Robert Evans, Parker Palmer, and the late Ted Sizer, to name some of the most influential.

Institutionally, I am deeply indebted to the Coalition of Essential Schools, the National School Reform Faculty, the Annenberg Institute of School Reform, Harvard College's Data Wise project, Heathwood Hall Episcopal School, Saluda County Schools, and Charlotte-Mecklenburg Schools (CMS).

I wish to publicly thank my mentors at the Coalition of Essential Schools: Jude Pelchat, Mary Hibert Neuman, Ted Hall, Paula Evans, Gene Thompson-Grove, and Joe McDonald.

Additionally, I would like to recognize my fellow Professional Development (PD) Coordinators at CMS: Barbara Ann Temple (Director), Meredith "Mary Parry" Parrish, Anne Gamblin, Angie Larner, Roxanne Breland, Joanne Whitley, and Renee Smith, as well as the rest of the Teacher PD Team. Cari Begin, formerly a PD coordinator with CMS, has been especially helpful in supporting various aspects of this work and continues to support me as director of the PLC Coaches Summer Institute. I am deeply grateful for her willingness and talent to help and for her unflinching confidence in me.

To my friends at Saluda Middle School (SMS) who have field-tested most of the ideas in this book, I wish to thank the amazing SMS principal, Shawn Love Clark, as well as Abbey Duggins and the rest of the SMS PLC coaches, and the former Director of Instruction for Saluda County Schools, Rosemary Patterson, who recognized my talents to help SMS in this process when time and money were limited.

Two individuals deserve the most credit in seeing this project to completion. Callouts to my wonderful editor at Corwin, Debbie Stollenwerk, whose great feedback and uplifting comments kept me staying the course, and my loving wife, Brady Evans, who would listen to my ideas and proofread chapters well past the point of being sick of hearing about PLCs, but who listened and read anyway.

PUBLISHER'S ACKNOWLEDGMENTS

Corwin gratefully acknowledges the following individuals for their editorial insight:

Diane Barone, Foundation Professor of Literacy Studies
University of Nevada, Reno
Reno, Nevada

Barrie Bennett, Professor
OISE/University of Toronto
Toronto, Ontario, Canada

Martin J. Hudacs, Superintendent
Solanco School District
Quarryville, Pennsylvania

Jadi Miller, Principal
Elliott Elementary School
Lincoln, Nebraska

Rosemarie Young, Principal
Watson Lane Elementary School
Louisville, Kentucky

About the Author

 **Daniel R. Venables** is founder and executive director of the Center for Authentic PLCs, a research and consulting firm committed to assisting schools in building, leading, and sustaining authentic PLCs. He is a Math/Science Fellow with the Coalition of Essential Schools and an award-winning classroom teacher of 24 years. He currently resides on a horse farm in South Carolina with his wife, Brady, their therapy dogs, Blue and Flo, and a cat named Fahrney. To invite Mr. Venables to your school, district, or event, contact him at dvenables@authenticplcs.com. To learn more about the PLC Coaches Summer Institute or the Center for Authentic PLCs, visit www.authenticplcs.com.

for Brady

Introduction

THE CALL FOR PLCs

In September 1980, the year I began my teaching career, I arrived early on the first day at Sorrington[1] High School, a public high school in the greater Hartford, Connecticut, area, for the first day of a two-day staff in-service. I don't recall any new teacher orientation in-service, as is customary now. Everybody showed up a mere two days before the students came. After the usual barrage of welcomes, announcements of weddings and new babies, introduction of new staff (which included me, a then baby-faced 21-year-old), OSHA film clips, insurance and benefits meetings, and such, I met individually with my immediate supervisor, Agnes Zorba,[1] who was the chairperson of the math department. During that meeting with Ms. Z (as the staff and students called her), I remember her handing me an Algebra 2 textbook and starting a conversation that went something like this:

Ms. Z: We cover Chapters 1–8, all of Chapter 9 except the last section, sections 10.1 and 10.2, all of Chapter 11 and, if you get to it, sections 12.1–12.3.

Me: Uh, okay.

Ms. Z: We're short one Teacher's Edition, but I've ordered one for you. Until it arrives, you'll have to work all the problems you assign for homework. You should do that anyway, just to be sure you know what's in store when you go over homework each day.

Me: Okay. I'll do that.

Ms. Z: And, as you map out the year tonight and tomorrow night, keep in mind that they have trouble with logs so allow a few extra days on that. I usually supplement logs with extra practice from other texts.

---

1. A pseudonym.

Me: Logs. Okay. Will do. Anything else I should know?

Ms. Z: Well, your sixth period class is a little large–I think 39 kids–so you'll have to run a tight ship. The Bartucci[1] twins are in that section.

Me: The Bartucci twins. Okay. Thanks for the heads-up.

And that was it. How I made it through the next two dozen years of classroom teaching remains a mystery to me. By necessity, I had to learn to do things myself. I learned by failing. I learned what not to do. I learned that the trig chapter was just as hard for them as the log chapter. I learned the hard way how the projects that I thought were so cool actually demonstrated very unsubstantial learning of my students. Why did I have to work in isolation? My seasoned colleagues already knew the lessons I learned on my own that first year. Why was there no mechanism in place for them to mentor me? How my learning curve could have shot up, more quickly, if there was a forum for me to learn from them and for them to also see fresh and new perspectives from me.

As Bob Dylan sang 16 years before that conversation occurred between Ms. Z and me, "Well, the times they are a-changin'" (Dylan, 2004). To be sure, teachers still work in isolation in significant part, but the closed classroom door of instruction is beginning to open. New teachers today often have their own in-service before the faculty at large returns from summer vacation, and many beginning teachers are assigned mentors to help them as they struggle during their first critical year. Even with such support, American public schools lose nearly half of their beginning teachers by their fifth year of teaching (U.S. Department of Education, National Center for Education Statistics, 2008).

Education in America is at a critical juncture. According to the National Assessment of Educational Progress (NAEP), the reading achievement of our 9-, 13- and 17-year-olds has flatlined in the past 20 years, with the scores for 17-year-olds actually dropping slightly in the past 10 years (NAEP, 2009b). Our math scores in these age groups have shown marginal increases but remain essentially unchanged (NAEP, 2009a). That would be disturbing enough, but the fact that this lack of improvement is happening in a context of an increasingly technological and complex world is worrisome. Global competitiveness in this flat world is no longer an advantage; it is a necessity for economic survival (Friedman, 2007).

As a nation, we are falling behind other first world countries in math and science. In fact, our best-performing states such as Massachusetts, Connecticut, New Jersey, and North Dakota are significantly and consistently out-performed on standardized eighth-grade math and science tests by countries such as Singapore, Taiwan, South Korea, Hong Kong, and Japan. Our lowest performing states in math and science have standardized scores for eighth graders that are comparable to eighth graders in developing countries such as Romania, Slovakia, and Estonia (NAEP, 2009a). As the 2007 Trends in International Mathematics and Science Study reports, eighth graders in the United States ranked 11th and 12th, respectively, in science and math among some 20 first world countries (TIMSS, 2007).

On the home front, we can still boast having the best colleges, universities, and medical schools in the world; however, we would be well advised to end any such conversation there. Our public K–12 schools that prepare students for those exemplary postsecondary institutions are falling dreadfully short. Our public schools face enormous challenges never before realized to this current critical extent. Challenges such as teacher shortages in math and science, increasing numbers of students living in poverty, the prevalence and influence of gangs in school neighborhoods, the deluge of English language learners populating our schools, and crippling budget cuts all contribute to the mosaic of obstacles that retard reform initiatives and as a result, any real improvements in teaching and learning.

To say that schools need interdependent support among their faculties is an understatement. Nearly every other type of professional—architect, doctor, engineer, actuary, and lawyer—routinely practices within a team, so that the veterans and the apprentices both maximize the quality of their work. It's high time we do the same in education. There is so much wisdom present amidst a group of teachers sitting around a table discussing teaching and learning. How can we tap into it? How can we structure ourselves so that we might break down the walls of isolation and work together to improve what we do and increase the learning of our students? The answer lies in schools implementing effective, collaborative teams of teachers.

This book is about how schools can build and sustain authentic PLCs that center around the teachers themselves to develop the skills and culture in which effective, accountable team collaboration can occur. That's not to imply that PLCs are a panacea for all things not working in schools, but it does imply putting student learning and student success above all else. It means setting our teacher egos on a distant back burner and doing whatever it takes to provide the best educational experience for all kids. It means working together to take a hard look at what we do, to converse openly and honestly about our work, and the effect of our work, and it means deliberately *planning* to impact student learning.

By their very design, PLCs function in a manner consistent with this notion and are, as Mike Schmoker says, the "surest, fastest path to instructional improvement" (Schmoker, 2006, p. 106). If we step back and think about it in a commonsensical way, we quickly come to the realization that when we provide teachers the *time, tools,* and *power* to work together to *analyze* and *alter* their *collective* and *individual* teaching practices, their students invariably benefit.

Just because PLCs make good sense doesn't mean that doing them well is easy stuff. Indeed, even the fastest and surest design eventually boils down to hard work (DuFour, Eaker, & DuFour, 2005). It's not enough for schools to simply have PLCs; they must do them well. I wrote this book to inform school leaders about how to do PLCs well, so that the presence of authentic PLCs in any school can make a difference in how much and how well students learn.

OUT WITH PROGRAMS, IN WITH PEOPLE

Many school leaders and policymakers, often desperate to increase student achievement and to do so in the shortest possible amount of time, simply cannot resist the allure of adopting well-pitched programs to fix their schools' problems. Just ask any teacher who has been teaching in the same school for the past five years. Ask her to list all the programs and initiatives her school has adopted during those five years and then ask her which of these will be promoted financially and supported administratively for the upcoming school year. I have no doubt that the list will shrink considerably, as principals let last year's programs, once the end-all in solving student achievement problems, wither and die in favor of this year's next "good program" that these well-meaning principals oblige upon their weary faculties.

I see several reasons for this. First, it is a reflection of America's general obsession with consumerism. If something is broken, be it our dishwasher or a wayward teenage son, we invoke a knee-jerk desire to buy something that will fix it and make our headache (in the case of the dishwasher) or heartache (in the case of our troubled teen) go away.

Second, and this is quite possibly related to the first reason, schools are often in denial regarding the complexities of their problems and want—often desperately—to believe that the latest brand name initiative or program, once adapted, will nearly effortlessly solve the problem of low student achievement. As if it were that simple.

And third, we are drawn to any program that promises a quick fix. And though, in all my visits to schools I have never met a principal who did not care deeply for the students in her charge, principals' jobs are often on the line. Many believe they can't afford to wait a year or two to see significant gains in student achievement. Some insist they can't afford to do the messy and longer work of developing their faculties to become effective collaboration teams and exceptional classroom teachers when the latest brand *du jour* promises quick results that claim to be "teacher proof." It is my constant battle cry throughout this book that, truth be told, principals cannot afford to *not* do these things.

Doug Reeves, in his recent book, *Transforming Professional Development Into Student Results,* offers sensible and compelling arguments why most programs are short-lived, far too plentiful in number, promote an acute lack of school focus, promote what he refers to as *Initiative Fatigue*, and just don't work in an undeniable majority of cases (Reeves, 2010):

> When the software licenses expire, the three-ring binders are lost, and the training is long forgotten, teachers will continue to have students walk into the classroom. Administrators will continue to work with teachers who need support and encouragement. In these many moments of truth, it will be people and the professional practices they carry with them, not the brand names, that define success or failure. (Reeves, 2010, p. 44)

People, not programs, are at the apex of serious school improvement and they are the nexus of authentic PLCs. It is not about brand name programs—whether they are implemented "with fidelity"—that matter most. It's about using to the fullest extent the talent and wisdom of a collective, an existing faculty of teachers that can, with intense and sustained focus on a few important things, bring about the most significant change and improvements in student learning.

Lest I give the impression that all well-pitched, well-advertised programs are bad or otherwise ineffective, let me say this: Some are indeed very good; the results they boast are valid and noteworthy. But it all comes down to people—the teachers who would implement (or not) these "researched-based" programs. I endorse no program. What I do endorse are faculties of teachers working together on a few specific tasks that, when done well, stand to make an enormous difference in what teachers do, how they do it, and in what kids learn. Read on, dear reader. The rest of this book is about what to focus on and how to focus on those few important things.

But first, let us consider where PLCs originated, what they are and are not, and how doing them well requires a seismic shift in teacher culture.

PART I

THE CONTEXT
FOR AUTHENTIC PLCs

1

The Business of PLCs

PLCs IN CONTEXT

The Evolution of PLCs

It's impossible to pinpoint exactly, but an argument could be made that the earliest incarnation of PLCs came from the work of Ted Sizer and the Coalition of Essential Schools (CES) in the late 1980s. They were called Critical Friends Groups (CFGs) back then, not PLCs, but they were based on many of the same guiding principles: groups of 6–12 teachers meeting regularly to look at teaching and learning in ways that improve their craft through focused dialogue and honest examination of their work and the work of their students. I was part of CFGs back then, trained to coach a CFG, and later assigned to train other coaches to lead their own CFGs. The work was rewarding and challenging and I learned many lessons along the way about what made these groups most effective.

Teachers who were members of CFGs back in the early 1990s learned quickly the advantages of being part of a collaborative team. They learned how carefully facilitated, structured mechanisms in place for honestly examining student and teacher work fostered growth in the teachers and improved the learning of their students. These mechanisms were greatly influenced by the work of Joe McDonald and Steven Allen (who replaced Grant Wiggins as senior researcher for CES), who designed the now famous Tuning Protocol for looking at student and teacher work. From there many other protocols came to be, and CFGs spread throughout the nation as ways to make a real difference in student achievement and teacher practice (Nave, 2000).

When No Child Left Behind (NCLB) legislation passed in 2001, state testing became the focus of every school, every principal, and by default, every teacher. CFGs that were born of CES were still widespread and active, but the emphasis morphed from student *learning* to student *performance* on state exams. Somewhere in the mix, the value of teachers working collaboratively on examining and improving their craft took a back seat to the drive to raise test scores—as if the two were mutually exclusive. Teachers returned to a competitive rather than cooperative mentality for survival reasons. The value of collaboration dropped to a low priority. In time, this isolation began to change and books by Mike Schmoker and Becky and Rick DuFour reminded us that real improvement in student learning happens best in the context of what became labeled *Professional Learning Communities* (DuFour & Eaker, 1998; DuFour, DuFour, & Eaker, 2008; Schmoker, 2006). Teachers and administrators once again came to believe that an increase in student achievement on state tests was inexplicably linked to teachers working together.

Here we are a decade later, knowing that PLCs—when done well—can change the way teachers do business and really make a difference in student learning, whether they measure that difference by state tests or by what teachers learn about their kids, independent of state tests. Arguably, PLCs can be the most efficient, least costly way of improving student learning. One reason for this is that PLCs act as a job-embedded source of sustained professional development for the teachers who would be part of them.

The Job of PLCs

PLCs exist to improve student learning by making teachers more effective in the work of teaching. In *Learning by Doing: A Handbook for Professional Learning Communities at Work*, Rick DuFour and colleagues outline three Big Ideas of PLCs: *Focus on Learning, Building a Collaborative Culture*, and *Focus on Results* (DuFour, DuFour, Eaker, & Many, 2006). The authors go on to identify six Essential Characteristics of PLCs that in part restate the three Big Ideas, adding[1] to the mix *Shared Vision, Collective Inquiry*, and *Commitment to Continuous Improvement* (DuFour et al., 2006).

Together, the three Big Ideas and the six Essential Characteristics provide the necessary mindset for schools attempting to establish effective PLCs. But when schools cherry pick the Big Ideas and Essential Characteristics in isolation without careful examination of the rest of the context and contents provided by DuFour, they can have widely variant views of the meanings of terms like *Building a Collaborative Culture, Focus on Learning*, and *Focus on Results*. When this is the case (as it has been in my experience), these terms become vague notions and merely add to our educational vernacular, joining the abstruse ranks of terms like *rigor* and *shared leadership*.

---

1. In proper chronology, DuFour started with the six Essential Characteristics and boiled these down to the three Big Ideas (DuFour, 2008).

Schools needed, in my experience working with them, to know what they should be doing, to *Focus on Learning* and *Focus on Results*. What did these focus points look like when they were played out in real schools? What did teachers do, exactly, and how did they do it?

To provide more traction to the ideas behind and characteristics of authentic PLCs, I suggest three *Essential Tasks of Authentic PLCs* to help schools narrow their focus:

1. Looking at student and teacher work

2. Designing quality common formative assessments (CFAs)

3. Reviewing and responding to data

Although PLCs may be continually engaged in these tasks, simply doing so may be insufficient in identifying a team as an authentic PLC. The *how* and not merely the *what* define PLC authenticity and we'll explore the *how* later. For now, let's examine how the Big Ideas align with the three Essential Tasks. Figure 1.1 shows how DuFour's three Big Ideas fit seamlessly with the Essential Tasks.

To be sure, it is possible for schools to have PLCs of limited or questionable authenticity and yet still be involved in looking at student work, writing CFAs, looking at data, and so on. If a teacher team is an authentic PLC, it generally follows that the teachers are engaged in certain tasks

Figure 1.1   Essential Tasks of Authentic PLCs and DuFour's Big Ideas

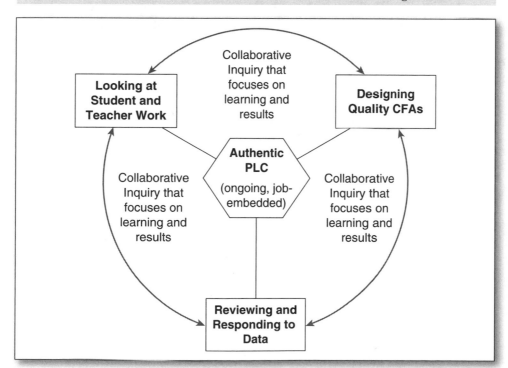

(the Essential Tasks); however, the converse is not necessarily true. Being engaged in the tasks, while necessary, is an insufficient condition for characterizing the teacher team as an authentic PLC. As we'll see in subsequent chapters, there is more to each of these Essential Tasks than meets the eye. Reviewing and responding to data, for example, means more than a cursory review of End-of-Year state test scores. Instead, it favors an ongoing practice that subscribes to the notion that data are vastly more abundant and continuous than the one-shot summative ilk of state assessments. Accordingly, so must be our use of that data in order to make important instructional decisions. Likewise, looking at teacher work implies more than individual teachers sharing what they're working on without a culture or mechanism for offering serious feedback to one another. Designing quality formative assessments involves more than teacher teams coming together to edit a textbook-published chapter test. Quality formative assessments are standards-based and their creation impacts not only what teachers assess and how they do so but also how teachers grade students and keep track of student mastery in grade books. In any discussion of *what* happens in effective PLCs—the business of PLCs—it is imperative to keep in mind something that seems to continually escape the multitude of reform efforts to improve student achievement: There is an obscure difference between the *means* and the *ends*. Having PLCs, doing the work of authentic PLCs, is not the end in and of itself. The "doings" of PLCs are essentially a set of *means* that can positively impact the *end*, which is without exception to improve student learning. This may seem obvious, but, in assisting schools with this work, I have learned that this distinction is crucial if teachers are to keep their primary focus on *what is accomplished* in terms of student learning and not on *what is done* in the PLC.

The Culture of PLCs

Time spent in an effective PLC meeting is very often different from the time typically spent in other teacher meetings. It feels different, it looks different, and in many ways it is the first time teachers experience a professional meeting that is not chock-full of announcements and housekeeping items that in no clear way have anything to do with teaching and learning. PLCs are focused completely on student learning, have a tenor of real and honest dialogue, and refrain from divergent conversations. PLC meetings have an atmosphere of identifying, investigating, and solving problems related to learning. For this reason, PLCs are not so much a *thing* as they are a *culture*. They are a way of thinking. *Things* can be done—often quickly—but culture develops through time. Consider Figure 1.2 as it compares the modus operandi of PLCs to that of other typical teacher meetings.

Figure 1.2 PLC Meetings Versus Typical Teacher Meetings

	Typical Teacher Meetings	*PLC Meetings*
Sense of Purpose	Often Vague Usually Not Discussed	Clear Frequent Reminders
Style of Meetings	Faculty Meetings Department Meetings	Work Groups
Focus of Agenda	Often Housekeeping Often Announcements Sharing of Anecdotal Stories Sometimes Gripe Sessions	1. Student Learning 2. Collaborative Designing 3. Collecting and Responding to Data
Basis for Discourse	Being Cordial, Being Cooperative	Being Trusting Being Honest
Leader/Facilitator	Directs Speaks a Lot Answers Easy Questions	Guides Listens a Lot Asks Hard Questions
Participants	Often Complacent Usually Compliant	Interested Involved
Agenda	Fixed Mostly Dictated	Flexible Shared
Atmosphere	Commiserating	Problem Solving
Silence Due to . . .	Passive Disagreement or Passive Acceptance	Reflection Deep Thinking
Mentality	"How will this idea impact me?"	"How will this idea impact student learning?"
Time Together	Mostly Self-Contained, Often Isolated	Ongoing, Sustained, Connected
Questioning and Disagreeing	Tacitly Discouraged	Openly Embraced
Attitudes That Are Valued	Being Positive Conforming	Always Being Truthful, Getting Results
Collaboration	Too Often Superficial	Essential
Decision Making Litmus Test	What's Good for the Teachers	What's Good for the Students

Many of the characteristics listed in Figure 1.2 are cultural in nature. They exemplify a shift in teacher culture, one that de-emphasizes isolation and individual teacher ego in favor of a culture in which goal-oriented, honest collaboration replaces the status quo.

MEETING LOGISTICS

When, How Long, and How Often

PLCs can vary widely in their size and makeup but the ideal size of a PLC is somewhere around six to eight teachers. Many PLCs work fine with as few as four teachers or as many as twelve. If the number of participants falls below four or climbs above twelve, the group's dynamics make the work more challenging and generally less productive. PLCs that are too small or too large suffer from a deficit or excess of varying perspectives (see *Establishing PLC Teams*, Chapter 2).

For teachers to adequately benefit from being in a PLC, I recommend teams meet at least weekly, for at least an hour each time. If the meetings are less than an hour—even though PLC meetings are characteristically focused—there is simply insufficient time to adequately practice protocols for reviewing student and teacher work and other tasks that require time. Additionally, most every meeting should end with a debriefing of the process, which is normally brief but requires time. Rushing the debriefing process or skipping it altogether retards the growth of the PLC toward efficiency. Joe McDonald has argued that if teams don't have time to debrief protocols, then they don't have time to do them (McDonald, Mohr, Dichter, & McDonald, 2007).

Many PLCs meet during teacher common planning times built into the school schedule, since common planning has become widespread in school districts nationally. Provided these periods are 60 to 90 minutes in length, this is the ideal time for PLCs to meet. If periods are shorter, as in some elementary and middle schools whose periods are closer to 45 minutes in length, it may be best to have PLCs meet immediately after school twice or three times a month for 60 to 90 minutes. Of course, as every classroom teacher will attest, teachers are understandably exhausted by the end of the day and the prospect of a PLC meeting after a long day of teaching—however valuable they may regard the meetings—is tiresome. Several districts in which I consult have adopted early dismissal days for students twice a month, providing PLCs the afternoons on these days to delve more deeply into their work. The decision to adopt such a schedule is one made by the principal and doing so communicates loudly and clearly to the staff that this work is a priority, so important that the normally static schedule is worth modifying to accommodate PLCs.

In short, PLCs should meet during the school day if possible when time is sufficient and after school when it is not. PLCs should meet no less frequently than once a week. Keep in mind that those PLCs that meet several times a week stand to progress several times faster than those PLCs meeting only once a week.

Agendas

As noted previously, PLC agendas differ significantly from agendas that characterize other types of teacher meetings. PLCs generally (1) begin with some review of the group's norms (see Chapter 2); (2) hear an update from persons who may have presented work at the last meeting, sharing changes implemented based on the feedback received at the previous meeting; (3) proceed with some task-experience such as the following: looking at student work using a protocol, problem-solving a teacher dilemma or issue using a protocol, engaging in a text-based discussion, writing a common assessment, reviewing data, designing a plan for instructional intervention, or designing a common lesson or unit; and (4) close with a debriefing of the process that occurred during the task-experience. The debriefing process is generally followed by a short discussion about the agenda for the next meeting (e.g., who will bring student work, who will follow up on which items, what homework or reading will be completed for next time, etc.). Figure 1.3 summarizes how a typical 60-minute PLC meeting might be organized.

THE ROLES OF THE PLAYERS

The Principal and Assistant Principals

First and foremost, principals must be 100% committed to making effective PLCs at their schools a top priority. Most every other district initiative and most other programs being implemented at the building level can be done within the framework of PLCs. PLCs are not an add-on to already full plates; they provide the structure for effectively dealing with most of the other stuff on the plate. Principals must embrace this notion.

If the faculty senses an insincere belief on the part of the principal that PLCs can really make a difference, the PLCs are doomed to fail. Worse, without clear and decisive support, the faculty will very likely corrupt the PLC experience and actually come away with the point of view that PLCs are just another top-down decision that has no significant impact on student learning and achievement. Once this happens—as it typically has in many schools with previous failed initiatives—it is difficult to go back and "do it right." For this reason, it is imperative that principals believe in the potential of PLCs. They must understand that as instructional leaders of their schools they are building capacity in their faculties to work together in an honest and collaborative way to really impact student achievement.

With the exception of leading the Coaches PLC (CPLC), principals generally do not participate in the individual PLCs. Of course, principals should and normally do attend the meetings of individual PLCs in their schools. This is part of their support. But while attending individual PLC meetings, they should sit on the sidelines and observe and refrain from participating within the groups. There are important reasons for this. Principals who constantly interject their thoughts while the PLC does its work stand to retard the very capacity the principals are trying to build in their faculties. If the principal does engage in this

Figure 1.3   Typical 60-Minute PLC Agenda

Activity	Description/Examples	Time Allotted
Review of Group Norms	Norms are read aloud. One reader per norm. Periodically norms are announced from memory.	2 minutes
Previous Presenter Update (if applicable)	"What changes/modifications have been implemented since the feedback from the last meeting? How are they working?"	2 minutes
Task-Experience **Notes** *Many of these tasks are done using protocols (protocols are explained in detail in Chapter 3).* *Some tasks are ongoing and others are self-contained.* *Some tasks require less time and can be grouped with other shorter tasks in the same 60-minute time period (e.g., doing a text-based discussion and also updating norms).*	• Review/Update Group Norms • Text-Based Discussion • Looking at Student Work • Looking at Teacher Work • Problem-Solving Issue/Dilemma • Reviewing Data • Designing a Lesson/Unit • Writing a Common Formative Assessment • Designing Instructional Intervention • Planning Action Research • "Unpacking" State Standards • Deciding "Power" Standards (Essential Learning Outcomes) • Peer Observation Visits • Peer Observation Conferencing	50 minutes
Debrief	Discussion of the process used to work on Task-Experience: *What worked well? What might work better?*	3 minutes
Next Agenda	• Who will present next time (if applicable)? • Follow-up responsibilities • Homework or reading to be completed prior to next meeting • Next steps in continuing today's work or goal for next meeting	3 minutes

kind of direct leadership, the PLC soon grows dependent on the principal to move the group forward and teachers in the PLC fail to grow dependent on one another. True PLC collaboration means that members become increasingly dependent on fellow members in making decisions, gaining insights, and solving individual and collective problems related to teaching and learning.

But what if, while principals are observing these PLCs, they have insightful input ("burning comments," as one principal called them) to contribute? The only time principals should be heard from is after the PLC, under the leadership of a capable coach, has fully debriefed the meeting or protocol as a group. Only then should principals share those insightful comments. This is how principals build capacity in their faculties: by letting PLCs "have at it." PLCs need to build shared experiences and knowledge with which to explore their teaching and the learning of their students. For some principals who are more comfortable directing rather than watching and listening, this new role is a challenge. (To help this, I suggest that principals who are observing a PLC meeting physically sit away from the group, in the "outer" circle, so that their presence does not in any way jeopardize the level of trust and honesty that is being developed or has been established by the group.)

Principals have much to gain from abiding by this, and they quickly acquire comfort with a more passive leadership role as they begin to see their faculties grow into self-assisting, interdependent teams of teachers.

The PLC Coach

Notwithstanding the importance of the principal's support and his leadership role in the CPLC, the role of the PLC coach or facilitator is paramount to the success of the PLC. It is in their delicate care that PLCs tend toward effectiveness or tend toward superficiality. Coaches are charged with the challenging but doable task of keeping the PLC moving forward, constantly weighing the needs and readiness of the group as a whole with the needs and readiness of individual group members. Coaches walk that fine line between uniting the group and pushing members to ask and answer the hard questions of each other that are inherent in any honest and authentic dialogue revolving around student learning. Through focused examination of teacher and student work, realistic analyses of available data, and responding to what the data reveal, coaches lead the group to improvement that transcends the benefits characteristic of the usual barrage of less effective professional development opportunities.

The credo of an authentic PLC is engaging in honest dialogue about what is happening in the classroom and what is needed to happen. The interest of participants in feeling good and speaking anecdotally and superficially about student learning becomes less important than their pursuit of having authentic dialogue. Teachers who are a part of an effective PLC know that the time for teacher "show & tell" is over; it is time to dig deeper and look constructively and collaboratively at what teachers do and explore the hard questions: Is this working? How will this improve student learning? This is the beacon for all PLC discourse and it is these questions, constantly raised and addressed by a capable PLC coach, which will make a difference.

Fortunately for those selected to coach these groups, there are ways to facilitate authentic dialogue. Procedures and strategies to effectively coach an authentic PLC are fully discussed in Part III.

The Participants

Let's face it: The participants in PLCs are ordinary teachers who have been asked (told?) to be members of a PLC. They may be willing to do the work, but in all honesty, they may have no real idea of what it is they're being asked to do. That's okay. If the principal and coaches do their jobs, participants begin to understand that PLCs cut through the familiar experience of meetings marked by general housekeeping, calendar notices, and ineffective conversations about teaching and learning. Teachers quickly appreciate the focus and productivity of PLCs, and they become a stronger faculty in general as they work deliberately in trying to improve their craft and help other teachers improve. With a little experience, participants routinely report their impatience with other teacher meetings, commenting that these other meetings are often "distractions" that stray from the real goal of improving learning. When this happens, it's a sure sign that the PLCs are working well and that they have taken hold of a new teacher culture in the school. This is inevitable; PLCs done well change expectations in the way teachers talk about school. What was once the status quo for teacher discourse becomes transparently inert.

That said, teachers in PLCs vary widely in their initial embrace of the work, their acquired appreciation of the work, and the extent to which the work of the PLC positively transforms their own teaching and assumptions about learning. In Chapter 6, we explore these differences in teacher PLC-readiness and offer insights and strategies for coaches to deal effectively with all of the teachers in their PLCs.

SUMMARY: PLCs

PLCs have been around for almost two decades, and while they are not a new idea, their recent popularity in schools is. When PLCs are authentic, the teacher culture of a school shifts from one of teachers working in isolation and competition to one in which teachers not only collaborate effectively but grow interdependent on each other, improving their individual and collective effect on learning.

PLCs can be structured a variety of ways; some teams are subject-specific, others are grade-specific (and therefore interdisciplinary). In fact, in many schools, teachers serve as members of both types of PLCs. Ideally, in a school whose culture is truly collaborative, every teacher meeting is a PLC meeting.

The time when PLCs meet is also varied, with most schools having common planning times in the daily schedule for PLCs to do their work. And when PLCs do meet, they are characteristically focused on teaching and learning and refrain from divergent teacher talk that detracts from this focus. Teams use protocols routinely, aiding in their effort to collaborate in open and honest ways.

Principals are key players in making PLCs a priority at their schools. Their leadership is passive, and principals routinely lead by example as they facilitate their own PLC made up of the coaches. The prevailing attitude on the part of the principal, and one that trickles down to the entire faculty, is that PLCs are serious work that can and will make a difference for the students who are served by the school.

2

What to Do First

Building a Foundation for Collaboration

BUILDING THE TEAMS

There are a plethora of reasons why a teacher team is dysfunctional rather than effective. One of the primary reasons is that the process is rushed; teams of teachers are given the title "PLC" by a well-intentioned principal and the tacit expectation is that teams jump into the work of PLCs (examining student work, writing assessments, looking at data, etc.). The problem is not the team's willingness to focus on these important things. The problem is that they have skipped an important step that lays the groundwork for those important tasks to be done well. When this happens, meetings typically plod along on the surface and participants never mention the elephant in the room, the fact that their endeavors are likely superficial dabblings in genuine PLC work. It is as if everyone knows the team is not effective, but no one will make an attempt to bring this obvious but unmentionable truth out in the open. The result is dissolving to the initial interest of being a PLC in the first place—to genuinely impact student learning. The extensive research of Bruce Joyce and Beverly Showers established that teacher risk-taking and growth follow not so much from teachers learning a new theory, but from the relationships teachers have with other teachers that center on mutual trust (Joyce & Showers, 1995). It's easier to form a team than to be one.

This lingering problem of relative ineffectiveness—common even with established, if ill-informed PLCs—can easily be circumvented by teams taking the time to build a *collaborative culture* before rushing into the tasks of authentic PLCs. In this chapter, we delve into things that PLCs can (and should) do to build a collaborative team. First, it is important to discuss the logistics of how to form the teacher teams and how to select coaches to lead them.

Establishing PLC Teams

The composition of teachers in a PLC depends on many factors and therefore takes on a host of configurations. Some of the factors influencing the PLC makeup include the school's grade levels (elementary, middle, high), the percentage of teachers in the school who are participating in PLCs, the subjects taught, the personalities involved, the time of day the meetings occur, the size of the school, the size of the district, the existence (or not) of subject-specific departments, and so forth. Knowing the context in which PLCs are to happen, it is the job of school administrators to decide how they will configure their teams.

Most PLCs in middle and high schools are organized by subject, and most elementary PLCs are organized by grade level. Some middle schools have both; teachers serve on a subject-specific PLC and also on a grade-specific PLC. While it is a lot for teachers to bear, there are synergistic benefits of having teachers serve on both. Generally though, a useful rule of thumb is that if teachers are subject-specific in what they teach, then their PLCs are also subject-specific. Since writing common assessments will be a significant part of their work, it is important that teachers of like subjects work together. In elementary schools, teachers usually teach multiple subjects and therefore their PLCs are most often organized by grade level.

At one time or another, I have been in PLCs configured in just about every imaginable way: by subject, by grade level, by facilitator preference,[1] by principal assignment, and by random selection. There are benefits to all of these. It is enlightening, for example, to be a math teacher in an interdisciplinary PLC looking at a project a student did in Spanish class—both for the math teacher and the Spanish teacher. For example, the math teacher might offer valuable input regarding the rubric the Spanish teacher plans to use in scoring a project students do on the global cultural contributions of Latin Americans. At the same time, the math teacher may gain insights

---

1. This was an interesting experiment. The principal announced to the faculty who would be coaching PLCs that year (they had had PLCs for several years), and each coach had a sign-up sheet in the office with 10 spaces for names. Teachers signed up, choosing the coach. The principal and coaches thought the faculty "buy-in" would be highest if the groups self-formed this way. It worked well, except for the fact that the math folks flocked over to the only coach who taught math, throwing off the makeup of the other groups.

from the Spanish teacher about how to organize the components of such a project, an insight applicable to math projects. Diversity in perspective, especially when it comes to looking at student work, can force teachers to reflect on their assumptions and assignments. When all the teachers in the PLC are math teachers—which, more than any other department, math teachers seem to insist on—the thinking can revert to the traditions of the status quo and can be incestuous at times. If schools like the idea of subject-diversity in their PLCs, this structure can work fine as long as there are other subject-specific team meetings being held that permit writing assessments, looking at data, and so forth. If so, the subject-diverse PLC can focus primarily on the job of looking at student and teacher work.

A final point to make concerns what many districts call "related arts" teachers. The most common question I get from schools regarding PLC configurations is what to do with the music, physical education, art, business, technology, and health teachers. The temptation to throw them together in a sort of misfit PLC is alluring, but these teachers often have very little in common and sometimes resent being the oddball group. Still, the only practical alternative to grouping them together is to disperse them to the academic subject PLCs, either by having them choose membership in one of these PLCs or by principal assignment to one of these groups. Related arts teachers often have valuable insights to offer teachers in traditional subjects, especially where performance-based assessments are concerned, since related arts teachers routinely use these kinds of assessments. That is what they *do* all have in common; often their greatest value as a misfit group is to focus on performance-based student work. Either way, their inclusion in PLCs is never ideal and some schools have permitted related arts teachers to participate as an option, on an individual basis. Again, as is the case with so much of this work in the PLC realm, there is no single way to do things. Principals must consider their options and make decisions that work best for the school and faculty toward the goal of using collaboration as a means to improve teacher practice and student achievement.

Selecting Coaches and Establishing a Coaches PLC

As mentioned in Chapter 1 (see *The Roles of the Players*), few entities determine the long-term success of the PLCs in positively impacting student achievement as the coaches assigned to lead these PLC teams. Most everything authentic (or not) and effective (or not) in a PLC is a result of the coaches' deliberate influence on the team. Choosing the right people to lead these PLCs is among the most essential ingredients to PLC success.

Once the PLC teams have been configured, the principal and his immediate administrative team must carefully decide who will facilitate or coach the PLC teams. These teacher leaders will meet regularly in their own PLC, the Coaches PLC (CPLC).

The CPLC serves a vital role in the school culture. The coaches who comprise the CPLC all facilitate their own PLCs in the school and act as a PLC in their own right. They form a necessary support system which enables them to better lead their own PLCs. The CPLC engages in experiences as a group, such as having a text-based discussion or practicing a particular protocol that will later be replicated in the coaches' respective PLCs. Having the experience first with their fellow coaches—and thoroughly debriefing how things went afterward—provides them with the necessary guidance to try the same experiences with their own groups. Additionally, the CPLC can use protocols to troubleshoot obstacles faced by coaches leading their own teams. This exchange of common issues and solutions that has worked in one PLC provides all coaches the wisdom, strategies, and support that helps them in their PLCs, whether the issue is teachers' late arrival to meetings, teachers' failure to follow up on between-meeting responsibilities, or difficulties with a reluctant member of the group. All coaches in the CPLC stand to benefit from airing and addressing concerns raised at CPLC meetings. Often CPLC members grow most interdependent, with each coach eager to present and solve problems they are facing in their individual PLCs.

Generally, the principal or assistant principal leads the CPLC, but this is not always the case. Sometimes the principal asks one of the coaches to lead the CPLC. If this occurs, it is important that the principal or assistant principal still acts as a full member of the group. This not only allows the school administration to keep its hand on the pulse of PLC progress throughout the school, but it also sends the message to the faculty that "this is important work," so important that the principal makes time in his schedule to attend CPLC meetings.

Sometimes the teachers who are selected to serve on CPLC are department chairpersons, and often they are excellent classroom teachers themselves, but neither characteristic is required. What is essential is that they have good people skills, are open-minded and hardworking, and are well respected by their teacher colleagues. The fate of PLCs as effective groups of teachers working honestly in collaboration to improve student learning rests largely in their hands. They should be carefully selected and thoroughly trained. I dissuade principals from asking for volunteers to be PLC coaches, for as every principal knows, teachers who volunteer for things are not always the most capable. Principals need their best *people*—not always their best *teachers*—doing the work of a PLC coach.

As a guide for selecting teachers to coach PLCs, Table 2.1 identifies desirable and undesirable characteristics in PLC coaches.

Admittedly, few coaching candidates or teacher leaders possess all of these desirable qualities. Still, the items in Table 2.1 can provide guidance in what to look for and what to avoid in selecting worthy PLC coaches. Naturally, the coaches' pool will be limited by the makeup of the PLC

Table 2.1   Desirable and Undesirable Characteristics of Coaching Candidates

Desirable Coaching Characteristics	Undesirable Coaching Characteristics
• Strong commitment to the concept of PLCs	• Interest in power
• Hardworking and dependable	• Interest in serving ego
• Good judgment, common sense	• Interest in promotion ("resume fodder")
• Ability to hear all sides when viewpoints differ	• Tactlessness, insensitivity to others' feelings
• Willingness to the group's good above personal good	• Preference in answering questions rather than asking them
• Willingness to address hard questions with integrity	• Greater interest in talking rather than listening
• Sensitivity to the affective quality of group dynamics	• Value in being right over doing right
• Sense of balance between celebrating accomplishments and getting results	• Complacency with superficial results
• Willingness to lead by example (rather than by ego)	• Tendency or history of holding grudges
• Sense of humor (not taking self too seriously)	• Undue sensitivity to valid criticism
• Staying power in school or district	• Inability to hold information in confidence
• Credibility with teacher colleagues	

groups. If the PLCs are by subject (or grade level), there are only so many candidates who might coach the groups. But attention to who is best to coach the group is more important than who is the best teacher or who has been at the school the longest or any other criteria sometimes used by principals to select teacher leaders.

Team Building

Sometime in the mid-1980s, there was a push for what was labeled "cooperative learning." In essence, it called for teachers to put students into groups, presenting undeniable facts about how kids need to learn to work at tasks together and how teachers need to arrange their lessons in ways that foster the opportunity for kids to work collaboratively. Principals across the nation told teachers to put students in groups and teach them the value of collaboration. And so teachers obliged, and class-rooms everywhere were compliant with this notion. But in no time at all, teachers began to divulge to one another in faculty rooms and parking lots that this wasn't working, that the students became social or uninvolved in these groups.

The problem wasn't that cooperative work groups aren't a good idea. The research is clear that they are. The problem was that simply putting kids in a group does not foster true collaboration. The same is true for teachers. Teachers, like students, need to learn *how* to work together. The first step in learning to work together is to become a team—an entity unto itself that is more than the mere sum of the individuals who comprise the team.

For a PLC to be effective, teachers must have some common vision to improve teaching and learning. They must become a united whole, willing to put personal agendas aside for the good of the group, toward the goal of really improving teaching and learning. This happens by building a team, by validating individual voices within the group, and by each participant seeing the work as greater than—indeed, more important than—individual needs and concerns. It starts by team building.

In a zealous but admirable rush to get on with the work of authentic PLCs, teams often dismiss the value of team building as either optional or too "touchy-feely" to be a necessary use of their cherished time together. Nothing could be further from the truth. In fact, large corporations routinely use team-building components in the training of their busy executives for the very reason that developing human capital is a worthy investment if teams are to function effectively. Indeed, the team-building activity I recommend and outline in Figure 2.1 derives from the business—not educational—community.

In my experience, good team-building activities provide three clear benefits to the PLC team:

1. Good team-building activities usually require the team to complete a particular task that necessitates a degree of interdependence that is characteristic in authentic PLCs.

2. Good team-building activities allow for a degree of fun and levity by participants.

3. Good team-building activities are often metaphorical in symbolizing the interpersonal dynamics of PLCs.

Traffic Jam, a team-building activity described in Figure 2.1, acts as all three.

Having used this team-building activity with many beginning PLCs (as well as with a fair number of students), I have never known a group not able to solve it. The time required will vary, of course, but in all cases

Figure 2.1

Traffic Jam

A team-building activity that mirrors the characteristics of a PLC.

Time allotted: 45 minutes (25 minutes for task, 20 minutes for debrief/discussion)

Materials: 7 mouse pads, cardstock paper, or masking tape to mark off the "stones"

Participants: 6 volunteers

There are seven stepping stones placed on the floor in a line, with spaces between them. On the three left-hand stones, facing right, stand three of the people. The other three people stand on the three right-hand stones, and face left. The center stone is not occupied to start.

The challenge: exchanging places

Participants move so that the people originally standing on the right-hand stepping stones end up on the left-hand stones, and those originally standing on the left-hand stepping stones end up on the right-hand stones, with the center stone again unoccupied.

The rules:

- After each move, each person must be standing on a stepping stone.
- Participants may only move forward, in the direction they originally face.
- There are two ways to move forward:
  - Participants may *jump* one person if there is an empty stone on the other side. Only one person may be *jumped,* and that person must be facing the *jumper.* (i.e., someone from the other side of three).
  - Participants may *slide* to an empty stone directly in front of them.
- If the group finds itself in a "traffic jam," participants must go *all the way back* to the starting position and try again. They may *not* simply redo the last few moves.

---

teams are eventually successful. That there is some difficulty, some starting over, some minor and temporary frustration is not only expected, it is desirable; therein lies some of the most important metaphorical parallels to life in an authentic PLC. It goes without saying that the discussion that follows *Traffic Jam* is essential. It is through this debriefing discussion that teams deepen their understanding of the elements of PLCs. Additional parallels to PLCs—some obvious and some more insightful—are included in a list of key discussion points for PLC coaches in Chapter 6.

Whatever team-building activity is used is less important than doing *some* team-building activity; its value in doing just that—building a team—should not be underestimated. If the activity also provides rich insights into PLC work, like *Traffic Jam* does so well, so much the better.

ESTABLISHING GROUP NORMS

In teaching teachers to work together to do the hard stuff of real collaboration, it is essential to establish a set of ground rules that govern all discourse. It is often too late to do this after problems within the group arise; by then, a degree of damage may have been done to the group and to the personalities within the group. The idea here is to be proactive rather than reactive. One meeting spent establishing group norms and subsequent meetings spent reviewing and reinforcing them will yield untold dividends down the road to becoming an effective, genuinely collaborative PLC.

Group norms are a set of mutually decided expectations regarding how meeting time will be spent, how disagreements will be addressed, and how all discourse among participants will be conducted. They range from norms such as "start and end on time" to "consider respectful disagreements" to "watch your air time." Teams decide norms together and doing so has the added bonus of team building in its own right. Participants hear each other's voices, complete with their pet peeves regarding teacher meetings, and this has the effect of uniting the team as members tacitly announce, "We need to know how you best function in this team for the very important work on which we are about to embark." For a PLC to skip this is for group members to start the PLC journey with one foot in the ditch. As Rick DuFour and others state in their expansive treatise on PLCs, *Revisiting Professional Learning Communities at Work,* "All groups will eventually develop norms. . . . In a PLC, rather than simply allowing norms to emerge, teachers reflect upon the norms that will make their collective experience more satisfying and rewarding" (DuFour et al., 2008, p. 284).

Of equal importance is for the group norms, once decided, to be reviewed constantly, at the start of each meeting. I suggest PLC coaches launch the start of meetings by asking a different teacher each time to read aloud the group norms. Nothing related to authentic PLCs is done once and forgotten. Until the norms become the culture of the group's meetings, they should be constantly reviewed and occasionally updated. All too often, well-intentioned PLCs dutifully decide group norms, only to never again refer to them or update them as they engage in the very tasks that require them. The result is a set of idealistic norms that are quickly forgotten and not actually abided by in team discourse. This sends the message that norms are a kind of hoop to jump through, without any relevance to the day-to-day goings on of team meetings.

Preamble to Setting Norms

There is a sort of catch-22 for teams writing their group norms that should be mentioned. The purpose of writing useful norms is to govern discourse at PLC meetings but in some sense requires teams to already be trusting, effective teams that are comfortable contributing to group discussions, disagreeing in earnest, and speaking up even when individual members find themselves in the minority. Yet, having group norms helps teams acquire this comfort, the comfort needed to write quality norms in the first place.

To help with this dilemma, I recommend that teams engage in two "feeder activities" that assist in encouraging honest, collaborative norm-writing in the absence of actually having norms with which to do this and in the absence of being an already established, seasoned PLC. The two feeder activities outlined here and taken in tandem act as precursors to the *Norm Setting Protocol* mentioned later. Together, they lay the foundational backdrop needed for the team to write thoughtful, useful group norms. There are no shortcuts to this; as DuFour and colleagues warn: "Beware of compromises that violate the fundamental premise and practices of a PLC" (DuFour et al., 2008, p. 416).

The first activity, *Compass Points* (see Figure 2.2), was developed by educators affiliated with the National School Reform Faculty (NSRF) and has been used by educators and business professionals for nearly 20 years. It compartmentalizes individual group styles into four broad designations (North, South, East, West) and, in doing so, raises awareness about the strengths and weaknesses of each style. The activity is engaging, humorous at times, and nonthreatening (with the possible exception of the propensity for three of the groups to announce the fourth as "most difficult to work with"). Participants work to answer questions along with members of their style; by constructing the task in this way, there is little room for that which is individually personal.

The second feeder activity, the *Peeves & Traits Protocol* (see Figure 2.3), is one I developed to provide the team with more personal information about individual styles while maintaining a nonthreatening environment. In my experience using it, the information participants learn about each other is nearly always eye-opening. During the first part of this activity, members indicate their pet peeves with regard to working in groups. During the second part of this activity, participants divulge some piece of information, not yet mentioned, that the group should know about them in order to work best with them in a group.

After the PLC has completed and debriefed the *Compass Points* activity, the group moves on to the *Peeves & Traits Protocol.*

Setting Group Norms

By the time the PLC has experienced both feeder activities, the team is well on its way to establishing group norms. Members have shared general and personal information about styles, preferences, and peeves related to working in a group. Alert coaches have made mental (if not written) notes of these, paying particular attention to how these preferences can be

Figure 2.2

Compass Points

An exercise in understanding preferences in group work.
Developed in the field by educators affiliated with the National
School Reform Faculty (NSRF).

Time: 35 minutes

1. The room is divided into four sections: North, South, East, and West.

2. PLC members are asked to place themselves at one of the four stations based on their style in working as part of a group (see below). It is worth noting that most teachers see themselves as some combination of these four; they should nonetheless commit to one that is most dominant in their style. (3 minutes)

North
Acting–"Let's do it."
Likes to act, try things, plunge in

West
Attention to Detail–Likes
to know the who, what,
when, where and how
before acting

East
Speculating–Likes to
look at the big picture and
possibilities before acting

South
Feeling–Likes to know that everyone's
feelings have been taken into
consideration and that their voices have
been heard before acting

3. At each Compass Point, the teachers answer the following and post their group responses on chart paper. (20 minutes)

   a. List three strengths of your style.
   b. List three limitations of your style.
   c. Which style do you find most difficult to work with and why?
   d. What do people from other styles need to know about you so you can work together effectively?
   e. What do you value about each of the other three styles?

4. The group of teachers at each Compass Point shares out to the large group. (12 minutes)

transformed into norms in the next activity. Members come to better know each other, often making remarks such as, "I had no idea that bothered you . . ." or "I really learned a lot about you guys. . . . I *thought* I knew you." By making these revelations, the team begins to not only know and

Figure 2.3

Peeves & Traits Protocol

Time: 20 minutes

1. Participants are each given an index card (5″ × 7″).

2. On one side of the card, participants write down *one* pet peeve they have regarding working in groups or at teacher meetings. They begin their pet peeve with the following phrase:

"It burns my butt when . . ."

(e.g., *"It burns my butt when people come late to meetings,"* or *"It burns my butt when people are interrupted during discussions,"* or *"It burns my butt when one person does all the talking,"* etc.) (5 minutes)

3. On the other side of the card, participants write *one* trait about themselves that everyone in the group should know about them in order to work best with them in a group setting. They begin their trait with the following phrase:

"One thing you all should know about me is . . ."

(e.g., *"One thing you all should know about me is that my silence is not due to disinterest; I just need process time,"* or *"One thing you all should know about me is I get excited during discussions and sometimes people are put off by my enthusiasm,"* or *"One thing you all should know about me is I am very visual and need to see on chart paper or on the Smart Board what we're discussing,"* etc.) (5 minutes)

4. Participants share both sides of their card in volunteer order without discussion (or elaborating on the card). (10 minutes)

---

appreciate style differences, but members come to appreciate the value in getting things out in the open—an ongoing practice in authentic PLCs. The writing of group norms after the use of the feeder experiences is typically more focused, more genuine, and less frustrating than attempting to write them at the onset, since many interpersonal preferences have already risen to the surface. Now it's time to distill those items down to a short set of useable, livable group norms (see Figure 2.4).

This protocol, coupled with the two feeder activities, produces quality group norms. In addition, it provides the opportunity for PLCs to verbalize public disagreements in Step 4. This is the beginning of acquiring comfort with such disagreements, and that will be essential to making high quality decisions in future work.

Policing and Reviewing Norms

It is not enough to have written group norms if they are never referred to again. The idea is that they are used and become integrated into the culture of how members of the PLC engage with each other. *The effectiveness of group norms is directly proportional to the willingness of team members to respectfully call each other on infractions of those norms.* Too often, teachers

Figure 2.4

Norm-Setting Protocol

Time: 60 minutes

1. The coach gives participants three index cards (5″ × 7″) and a black marker.

2. Writing on only one side of the card, participants write down *one* group norm they would like to see. No more than one norm per card; participants can write as many cards as they like. (5 minutes)

3. The coach collects all cards and randomly passes them out to participants. Each participant reads the cards she has been given and other participants share their card if theirs is the same or closely related to the one being read. As cards are read, they are collected by the facilitator and posted in groups of like norms (e.g., "respect," "disagreements," "agenda," etc.). Discussion is limited to grouping norms and identifying similarities between norms. (20 minutes)

4. *Dissent option.* After the coach posts all cards into categories (though some will be "stand alones"), participants can propose to eliminate any norm. If one other participant "seconds" the opinion that a particular norm be eliminated, the index card of that norm is removed. (5 minutes)

5. As a whole group, the facilitator leads a discussion of condensing each group of norms into a single norm (without stringing them all together with the use of "and"). The goal is to word a single norm that captures the essence of the group of like norms. (30 minutes)

6. *Next steps.* The facilitator asks for a volunteer to do whatever "wordsmithing" is still needed for the norms, after the meeting. The final product is a list of four to six group norms that will govern all discourse in the PLC. [I like to make a poster of the final list and have all PLC members sign the poster. It is then displayed prominently in the meeting room.] Hereafter, the group norms should appear at the bottom of each meeting agenda.

assume that the PLC coach owns the responsibility of "enforcing" the norms. When the PLC coach makes it clear that all members are responsible to "speak up" when members fail to adhere to the norms, it is easier for teachers to do so and less likely that doing so will result in hard feelings by those teachers violating the norms.

From time to time, group norms should be updated. Original norms may outlive their usefulness either because the norm itself was not practical and could not be abided by or because the norm has become so ingrained in the culture of the PLC that listing it as a norm seems silly. New norms, the need for which may not have been realized at the onset of the PLC work, might need to be added. All updates are done collaboratively by the whole PLC so that all voices are heard—including dissenters—and so each member owns the new list.

CONSTRUCTING COMMUNITY KNOWLEDGE

PLC members bring with them a history of career experiences and volumes of knowledge about teaching and learning. These experiences and lessons have shaped their teacher identity, style, beliefs, and assumptions as well as how they will process the next bit of new information and what they will decide to do with it. They see every new teaching and learning permutation based on this context of prior experience. The fact that PLCs are made up of *different* people, with *different* (although often similar) histories of experience provides a source of great team wisdom and also opportunities for members to have differing perspectives. This is a good thing. In addition to individual histories of experiences, in the time they spend together, the PLC will amass a *collective* history of experiences. This is more than the simple pooling of individual members' knowledge and experiences; this is a collection of common experiences and learning that the PLC acquires together, in real time.

The norm-setting experiences outlined earlier do more than set quality, thoughtful group norms and team build in their own right; they provide a valuable opportunity for PLCs to *construct community knowledge.* In the case of norm setting and sharing stylistic preferences in *Peeves & Traits,* the community knowledge the participants constructed had to do with individual styles in working collaboratively. Depending on the experience at hand, the community knowledge that is constructed will vary. Sometimes it is related to group styles and other times it may be related to learning about standards-based assessments or how to weigh dimensions in a rubric. When knowledge is acquired together and at the same time during a common experience by members of a PLC, that knowledge becomes the bedrock on which future shared understandings are built. For example, having had a text-based discussion regarding the limitations of multiple-choice items on assessments, the team is better equipped to discuss an assessment presented by a teammate during a protocol.

Conclusions and decisions made on the basis of having constructed community knowledge are embraced by the PLC; accordingly, resulting work is shared and owned by all members of the team. When members learn together and each is a part of the growing pains along the way, teams experience a higher degree of solidarity. Effective principals already know this; when faculties start on the same page at point A, derivative decisions and focuses at points B, C, and D make more sense and generally enjoy more teacher "buy-in" than when later points are handed to faculties by school leaders. A PLC that has discussed issues related to student tardiness to class, for example, is more likely to ask students roaming the hallways, "Where are you supposed to be?" than if doing so was merely mandated by a principal email. All of these things, rooted in having constructed community knowledge, contribute to the school as a whole, functioning as a united PLC.

In authentic PLCs, teams construct community knowledge and the effect of doing so builds the culture of collaboration that is essential for the important tasks ahead. At first, the community knowledge is about individual styles in working as part of an effective team. The triad of activities that culminated with usable norms accomplished this. Next in line are less interpersonal vehicles for constructing community knowledge that more closely align to the tasks ahead: experiencing *common readings* and deciding *Essential Learning Outcomes* (ELOs).

Engaging in Common Readings

Another way PLCs can construct community knowledge is to engage in common readings and discussions of those readings. Not only is this relatively easy to do, it provides several important benefits.

First, common readings produce common knowledge. In many ways, common readings and discussions about those readings put the "L" in PLC: *Learning.* By doing the readings and talking about the content that was read, PLC members learn together. The comments and insights that are shared deepen everyone's understanding of the text in a way that puts them all on the same page. The material knowledge gleaned from both the readings and the discussions can be and often are referred to in later work. Everyone around the table understands these references since they were all originally part of the construction of this community knowledge. Carefully selected readings are paramount to success. Teachers and schools that subscribe to ASCD's monthly publication, *Educational Leadership,* or Phi Delta Kappa's publication, *Kappan,* have a steady supply of quality, current material with which to engage PLCs in text-based discussions.

Second, common readings set a tone of seriousness and scholarliness. Engaging in them tacitly announces, *This is serious work. We all need to do some homework occasionally between meetings. We will always follow up on this homework, and we're doing this to learn more about X.* Often the readings that are chosen target specific areas in which the team needs to learn more. If the team is struggling with differentiating their instruction, needs strategies for reaching low achievers, is having trouble with assessments, or could benefit from the latest brain-based strategies, there are usually recently published articles or books that can help. It is important to note that these readings are not the more common "book studies" that have become popular with faculties. The choice of reading may be a chapter in a book, but it rarely involves reading and discussing a whole book (the book you hold in your hands notwithstanding). The most effective discussions are usually fueled by short articles or a few sections from a chapter in a book.

Third, common readings about PLCs can dramatically accelerate the PLC learning curve. Readings about CFAs, looking at student work, analyzing data, or about PLCs generally can help teams gain insights into their work and function as an authentic PLC. PLC coaches are advised to read about facilitation techniques (see Chapters 6 and 7).

Fourth, engaging in common readings and the essential discussions that follow strengthen the PLC as a collaborative team. Coaches sharpen their skills as they find themselves having to referee the group during discussions; members learn to contribute in more general, less autobiographical ways; and teams begin to respectfully disagree or gain comfort in sharing divergent opinions. All of these things unite the team as a collaborative whole—essential for the work that follows.

And finally, discussions of the readings are generally conducted by use of protocols and thereby provide the PLC with invaluable experience in using protocols. This experience and comfort with protocols yields dividends when the PLC later examines student and teacher work or looks at student data using protocols.

Deciding Essential Learning Outcomes

Once the PLC has engaged in team building, learned about each others' styles and preferences in collaborative work, established group norms, and shared the experience of discussing text from common readings, it's time to take a hard look at what team members will teach. This bedrock task begins by team members coming together, each with state standards[2] in hand, and deciding what to teach—or more pointedly, what *not* to teach.

State standards are notorious for being impractically comprehensive. The amount of material expected to be mastered by students is not only overwhelming to teachers, it is downright unachievable, unless teachers merely *cover* the material in a most superficial way. It has been reported to the point of cliché that U.S. curricula are "a mile wide and an inch deep." Dr. Robert J. Marzano remarked during a talk given at the 2007 ASCD conference that, based on his research, K–12 curricula in the United States is so overcrowded that students would need a K–22 program to learn it all (Marzano, 2007).

That the curricula must be trimmed is an understatement. But this is where things get tricky. Knowing intellectually that state content needs trimming and actually doing the trimming are vastly different things. Teachers cling to most every curricular topic—collectively, if not individually. Teachers all have their favorite topics to teach and discussions by subject-specific PLCs about what gets cut can become heated at times. (Indeed, this is all the more reason to precede this important discussion with the experiences outlined previously in this chapter.) Still, trim we must if students are to master the remaining topics with fidelity, the very fidelity demanded by state assessments.

Mere coverage of the material perpetuates the mindset that student *exposure* to topics somehow translates into student *mastery* of the topics.

---

2. At the time of this printing, the Common Core State Standards in mathematics and English language arts have recently been released and adopted by 48 states for Fall 2014 implementation. States will have the option to continue using their own state curricula and assessments if they choose. Either way, an important discussion prioritizing topics will be necessary, whether that discussion happens at the school, district, state, or national level.

We know from the weighty mass of brain research that true mastery—the kind required by most state tests—doesn't equate with simple coverage. In fact, "without rehearsal or constant attention," information that is merely covered is very soon lost, a phenomenon Patricia Wolfe refers to in her book, *Brain Matters,* as the "18-second holding pattern" (Wolfe, 2001). For mastery, students need repeated exposure to and practice with the topic in a way that builds through time (Wolfe, 2001). Teachers are beginning to realize that it's not what *we* do with the material (coverage); it's what the *students* do with the material (toward mastery).

As teacher teams face the tough decision of what gets cut and what topics are worthy of teaching in continued depth, I recommend that two criteria be considered:

> **PROMINENCE.** How prominent is this topic on the state End-of-Course (EOC) exam? How heavily weighted is this skill or concept in terms of percentage of items on the EOC assessment?
>
> **VITALITY.** How vital is knowledge of this topic to later skills or coursework? How essential is mastery of this particular skill to student success on later topics in this course or in future coursework?

To be sure, there are a host of other criteria that could be used in sorting topics and deciding which ones to emphasize (or teach at all). The longer the list of criteria, however, the more likely it is that nothing gets deleted. Therefore, I have found that these two essential criteria work well to filter topics based on what really matters: *How much of this is on the state test? Will kids need this later on?* Both criteria generally appeal to teachers for the reason that the criteria are grounded in common sense.

To assess objectives or substandards[3] in state curricula against these two criteria, I propose that each objective or substandard be scored according to the following rubric (see Figure 2.5). This rubric can be used as a litmus test for topic inclusion.

For each topic under discussion, PLC teams come to consensus and rate each substandard using this rubric. Then topics can be sorted and viewed graphically, by illustrating the location of each topic on the scatterplot in Figure 2.6.

By first scoring and then organizing topics in this way, PLC teams are forced to view curricular topics more objectively than would be possible by having a general conversation about what gets cut. The result

---

3. Nomenclature for "substandards" varies from state to state. For example, in North Carolina, the state has identified four or five *Goals* for each course and subgoals are called *Standards.* In South Carolina, each course is comprised of four or five *Standards,* and substandards are referred to as *Indicators.* Whatever the subgoals are called, each of these is measured using the rubric in Figure 2.5.

Figure 2.5   Rubric for Deciding Essential Learning Outcomes

	1	2	3	4
PROMINENCE	1%–3% of tested items	4%–7% of tested items	8%–12% of tested items	> 12% of tested items
VITALITY	not vital; isolated skill/topic	few connections to later work; can be taught "as needed" in later work	Important prerequisite skill/concept in this and later coursework; recurs with increasing depth	vital skill/concept; essential for success in later coursework; recurs frequently with increasing depth

is a newly trimmed curriculum, one trimmed on the basis of two important criteria (prominence and vitality) rather than on the basis of personal attachment to individual topics by individual teachers. By using the graphic in Figure 2.6, any topic not scoring a 3 or 4 on at least one of the two criteria is deemed nonessential. Thus, somewhere in the neighborhood of 20% to 25% of the topics listed in the state standards is omitted. This notion is difficult for PLCs; the thought of omitting topics that will be assessed on state assessments—even if only marginally—is counter to conventional thinking and hard for teachers to embrace.

Figure 2.6   Scatterplot for Sorting Scored Topics

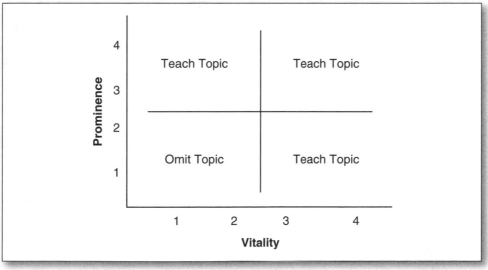

In *On Common Ground: The Power of Professional Learning Communities*, renowned educator and author Douglas Reeves (2005) writes, "Only a few states have prioritized standards, thus leaving a majority of teachers with two options: curriculum by default or curriculum by design" (p. 48). He goes on to say, "Curriculum by default is the result of the urgency with which we often act—we inevitably run out of time, energy, and patience by the end of the school year. Curriculum by design, however, reflects decisions made before the school year begins" (p. 49). Those decisions to which he refers are the ones authentic PLCs make in trimming the curriculum.

What makes this trimming sensible is that the time freed up by the omissions allows teachers to explore in greater depth those topics that are decidedly prominent and vital. It's a trade-off of sorts, but one that is necessary to move from teacher *coverage* to student *mastery*. When PLCs take a hard look at essential and nonessential learning outcomes, they begin to focus on what matters most. This focus will drive everything PLC, from looking at student and teacher work to designing quality CFAs. Only when PLCs are focused on ELOs can true improvement occur, both in terms of instruction and student performance. But to achieve this, PLCs must first have a necessary and difficult discussion about what gets cut.

When PLCs come together and make these hard decisions, they not only unite more strongly as a team, they are constructing community knowledge. For one thing, teachers gain detailed knowledge about the wording and interpretations of the state standards. They come to know the standards better by having experienced the scoring and sorting outlined previously. They also construct community knowledge about what is important to teach. This gets the team on the same page and clarifies a common vision for their students.

We will have other opportunities to construct community knowledge when we look at data in Chapter 5. For now, the point is that when teachers do not feel that they are empowered to make important decisions, and when important things are decided without them and handed down from well-meaning administrators, those decisions are rarely abided by except in most perfunctory ways. For example, I was asked in April 2010 to help a middle school starting to build authentic PLCs with its faculty. When I arrived, I learned that the school's eager principal, having read about effective collaboration, assigned a teacher task force to decide group norms for the entire faculty and their PLCs. It was no surprise to me to also learn that virtually none of the PLCs actually used or followed the norms. When important decisions like how meetings will be conducted or what to teach are decided by the team that will implement them, the teacher buy-in is significantly increased. Constructing community knowledge and deciding things based on that knowledge is part of the learning curve—indeed, part of the *learning*—of authentic PLCs.

SUMMARY: COLLABORATION

Being a team is not the same thing as forming a team. If I have learned anything about implementing authentic PLCs it is that the hard work of looking at student and teacher work, designing quality CFAs, and reviewing and responding to data cannot be done well without first building a strong collaborative team. There is no bypassing this. Time spent team building, learning about each other's styles and preferences in working as part of a team, norm setting, and constructing community knowledge is never time spent in vain. Quite the contrary; failure to do these things promotes dysfunctional, ineffective PLCs with members who, at best, go through the motions of engaging in the requisite Essential Tasks with little or no impact on student learning. With no real gains observed, inauthentic PLCs soon revert back to the old ways of the comfortable, if ineffective, status quo.

Once a solid, collaborative foundation is established, PLCs are ready to do the heavy lifting of looking at student and teacher work, designing quality CFAs, and reviewing and responding to data, and they stand a good chance of doing them with fidelity so that student learning can actually improve. Well-established teams can tackle any obstacle that may arise as they pursue the three Essential Tasks that follow in Part II ahead.

PART II

THE ESSENTIAL TASKS OF AUTHENTIC PLCs

3

Looking at Student and Teacher Work

After establishing group norms and immersing the PLC in activities that strengthen core values such as honesty and trust, it is time to move the focus from interpersonal dynamics to one more centrally targeted on student learning. Just as protocols guided the group through the process of establishing group norms and identifying individual styles, protocols are also suited for looking at student and teacher work. The values are much the same—honesty and trust—and the practice of PLCs collaboratively examining and discussing student and teacher work fosters continued growth in interpersonal team dynamics.

As mentioned in Chapter 1, the *Essential Tasks of Authentic PLCs* are as follows:

1. Looking at student and teacher work

2. Designing quality CFAs

3. Reviewing and responding to data

In this chapter, we focus on the first Essential Task: looking at student and teacher work. The research is abundant and its conclusions are both clear and not astonishing. In schools where teachers carve out time to meet and to honestly and collaboratively discuss the work produced by their students and their colleagues, an unsurprising thing starts to happen: The work gets better (DuFour, DuFour, Eaker, & Karhanek, 2004). Not only do students learn more, but also more students learn (DuFour et al., 2004). In many ways, looking collaboratively and closely at what we do and what students do is the bedrock of what it means to be part of a PLC.

But it doesn't just happen because we put teachers in a room together and say, "Ok, let's collaborate" or "Ok, let's all go around and say what we're working on with our kids." For teachers to engage one another in candid and in-depth discourse about what they are doing or what results their students have produced requires mechanisms that preserve the integrity of honest feedback while protecting the safety of the teacher presenting his work. Those mechanisms are protocols.

PROTOCOLS FOR STUDENT AND TEACHER WORK

Protocols as tools for examining student work sprung from the work of CES, a mid-1980s reform effort centered on the principles of Ted Sizer, outlined in his landmark book, *Horace's Compromise* (Sizer, 1984). The first and probably most used and significant protocol is the *Tuning Protocol,* written by David Allen and Joseph P. McDonald, both senior staffers at the time at CES. McDonald and Allen recognized the need for a structure within which teachers could honestly and safely look at each other's work. The *Tuning Protocol* came out in 1991, two years before my training with CES as a Math/Science Fellow. With remarkable success, Allen and McDonald created this mechanism that allowed teachers to present their work or the work of their students in a way that transcended the usual "Show & Tell" of teachers presenting work and encouraged honest discussion in a nonthreatening manner.

Allen and McDonald realized that a general discussion of a teacher's work by colleagues often found that well-intentioned and valid criticism (if offered at all) was often met with a degree of defensiveness on the part of the presenting teacher. As a result, valid points of question or concern were soon overcrowded by the discomfort of the critiquing teachers offering the feedback and by the inability of the presenting teacher to separate her work from her teacher ego. To alleviate this, they devised the *Tuning Protocol,* which spelled out who was to speak and when. They learned that by delaying when the presenter could speak and allowing the teacher to respond to points made by the feedback team, the presenter was not only less defensive, but she actually made changes in her work based on the points made. Accordingly, the teacher's work was more likely to improve based on the input. And, of no less importance was the fact that "cool" feedback was encouraged—feedback that points out gaps and makes suggestions—since the protocol is structured in such a way that there is time built in for offering such feedback. All members of the PLC gained from the experience. It was, in many cases, the first time teachers actually gave sincere feedback that actually helped a colleague improve, while at the same time protecting the "teacher ego" of the presenting teacher.

The value of the *Tuning Protocol* does not stop there for two very good reasons. First, the team of teachers involved in this process becomes more closely knit having been through the experience. Second, everyone around the table becomes to some extent a better teacher. Although all members focus their attention on one particular teacher and her particular students, it is impossible to be a part of this experience without reflecting—at least silently—on one's own teaching, one's own students, one's own assignments and projects. Case-study research done for CES on CFGs in the late 1990s showed that net gain of such groups was eye-opening and considerable (Nave, 2000).

Many more protocols have been created since 1991, all of which contain the spirit of the original *Tuning Protocol* by acting as mechanisms for teachers to collaboratively, respectfully, and honestly look at any piece of the complex jigsaw puzzle of teaching and learning. PLCs gain invaluable insights from such explorations and these insights ultimately translate into qualitative and quantitative improvements in student learning.

Protocols for conducting structured conversations among teachers about student learning have since been perfected and the rough spots and drawbacks of early protocol versions have been ironed out. Today, the protocols have been thoroughly "field tested" and those that remain are effective, efficient processes for honestly looking at what we do as teachers and how that impacts student learning. I suggest this to all PLCs beginning to implement protocols: trust the process. What initially may seem awkward or rigid becomes a comfortable way for teachers to be focused, honest, and helpful to each other. After a little experience, teachers routinely remark how much it has helped their practice and many look forward to their turn being in the "hot seat," presenting their work or the work of their students (Nave, 2000).

Some of the commonplace conversations that occur in customary team meetings are not acceptable discourse during protocols. Extraneous focus on tangentially related issues is not tolerated during a well-facilitated protocol and neither is focusing on oneself (as often happens in other teacher meetings) with comments like, "What I do is. . . ." or "I had this happen in my class. . . ." All eyes, ears, thoughts, comments, and ideas are focused on the teacher (or the team of teachers) who is presenting his work or the work of his students. This makes protocols fascinating to witness. It is as if for some 50 minutes, no one in the room cares about anything except the work of the presenting teacher and how he can be assisted to make that work better. In this chapter, I discuss three primary protocols for examining teacher and student work. I begin by looking at the *Tuning Protocol* whose steps are outlined in Figure 3.1.

Figure 3.1

Tuning Protocol

Developed by Joseph McDonald and David Allen.

1. Introduction (5 minutes)
   * Facilitator briefly introduces protocol goals, guidelines, and schedule
   * Participants briefly introduce themselves (if necessary)

2. Presentation (15 minutes)

   The presenter has an opportunity to share the context for the student work:
   * Information about the students and/or the class—what the students tend to be like, where they are in school, where they are in the year
   * Assignment or prompt that generated the student work
   * Student learning goals or standards that inform the work
   * Samples of student work—photocopies of work, video clips, etc.—with student names removed
   * Evaluation format—scoring rubric and/or assessment criteria, etc.
   * Focusing question for feedback
   * Participants are silent; no questions are entertained at this time

3. Clarifying Questions (5 minutes)
   * Participants have an opportunity to ask "clarifying" questions in order to get information that may have been omitted in the presentation that they feel would help them to understand the context for the student work. Clarifying questions are matters of "fact."
   * The facilitator should be sure to limit the questions to those that are "clarifying," judging which questions more properly belong in the warm/cool feedback section.

4. Examination of Student Work Samples (15 minutes)
   * Participants look closely at the work, taking notes on where it seems to be in tune with the stated goals, and where there might be a problem. Participants focus particularly on the presenter's focusing question.
   * Presenter is silent; participants do this work silently.

5. Pause to reflect on warm and cool feedback (2–3 minutes)
   * Participants take a couple of minutes to reflect on what they would like to contribute to the feedback session.
   * Presenter is silent; participants do this work silently.

6. Warm and Cool Feedback (15 minutes)
   * Participants share feedback with each other while the presenter is silent. The feedback generally begins with a few minutes of warm feedback, moves on to a few minutes of cool feedback (sometimes phrased in the form of reflective questions), and then moves back and forth between warm and cool feedback.
   * Warm feedback may include comments about how the work presented seems to meet the desired goals; cool feedback may include possible "disconnects," gaps, or problems. Often participants offer ideas or suggestions for strengthening the work presented.
   * The facilitator may need to remind participants of the presenter's focusing question, which should be posted for all to see.
   * Presenter is silent and takes notes.

7. Reflection (5 minutes)
- Presenter speaks to those comments/questions he or she chooses while participants are silent.
- This is not a time to defend oneself, but is instead a time for the presenter to reflect aloud on those ideas or questions that seemed particularly interesting.
- Facilitator may intervene to focus, clarify, etc.

8. Debrief (5 minutes)
- Facilitator-led discussion of this tuning experience.

In the same way teachers learn to trust this process in order to reap the benefits of an effective protocol, coaches must honor the process and adhere to the structure. It is essential that coaches be somewhat militant, especially at first, in laying the groundwork for participants to glean the most from the experience. PLC coaches must trust the process and insist that their PLCs adhere to it, despite the tendency for teacher groups to show some initial resistance to the formality of protocols. If coaches do so, their PLCs will grow fast both in terms of trust and effectiveness; if they do not, they risk their PLCs degrading into the multitude of ineffective, divergent teacher meetings to which educators have become accustomed.

McDonald and his colleagues (2007) explained the following in their book, *The Power of Protocols: An Educator's Guide to Better Practice*:

We read students' work closely and collectively for two reasons. One is to learn more about students' learning—to gain clues about their strengths and weaknesses, their misconceptions, their proximity or distance from a conceptual breakthrough, their progress with respect to some defined standard, or their unique way of thinking and working. We also read students' work closely as a text that captures the efficacy of our own work. This text is where our moves as educators and their impact on students are most traceable. It is where the strengths and weaknesses of our practice—individual and collective—become the most apparent. Thus our efforts to explore student work together are crucial to our efforts to revise and improve the collective work of our educational institutions. For these reasons, however, looking at student work—particularly looking together at student work—can be threatening. This is why protocols are useful. They protect us from what we may perceive as social danger, even as they teach us habits we wish we already had. (p. 4)

As participants learn to trust the process and as facilitators steadfastly insist on sticking to it, members of PLCs come to appreciate the effectiveness and efficiency of using protocols. Thereafter, it is not uncommon for such groups of teachers to desire and expect all serious teacher conversations and problem-solving meetings to use protocols.

Later in this chapter we delve into how PLCs use protocols, which ones they should try first, and which protocols work best for various aspects of teacher and student work as well as for the dilemmas and issues faced therein. For now, it is important to consider the role and importance of giving and receiving feedback.

FEEDBACK

In some form or another, feedback is the lifeblood of nearly every aspect of PLC work, most notably, the lifeblood of looking at student and teacher work. It is the traction needed under the slippery wheel of collaboration. The quality of teacher discourse in an authentic PLC depends in large part on the quality of the feedback teachers are willing to give and receive from one another. If the feedback given during the examination of student work is only limited to surface comments and fails to dig deeper into the work, the quality of the improvements of the work will be similarly limited and the time spent discussing the work will have, for the most part, been in vain. It is the purpose of this section to examine types of feedback and offer tips for giving and receiving useful feedback.

Teachers are not in the habit of offering critical feedback to one another. Even teachers who routinely work in teams rarely offer serious feedback. If and when teachers share work, it is commonplace for the work to be shared in a "Show & Tell" format where comments made about the work—if they are made at all—rarely stray from celebratory, complimentary comments. Teachers are generally more likely to offer thunderous applause at the conclusion of the sharing than to offer a single critical comment. In my work with teachers, I see four primary reasons for this:

1. Teachers do not offer critical feedback because they are worried about appearing "negative" to the rest of the group. This is especially true if the established culture of sharing is generally celebratory in nature.

2. Teachers do not offer critical feedback because they are worried about hurting the feelings of the teacher who is sharing work. The presenting teacher may get defensive and she may resent the feedback after the meeting is over. It is not worth jeopardizing the professional relationships involved; it is easier and safer for participants to be positive and avoid offering critical feedback.

3. Teachers do not offer critical feedback because they are not thinking deeply about the work being shared. It is easier to be complacent and keep concerns about the work to oneself. Teachers may have little or no investment in the work being presented or in actually helping the presenting teacher. Giving critical feedback is not

only risky, it demands that we think deeply about the work of a colleague.

4. Teachers do not offer critical feedback because there is no format or structure with which to do this. There are no rules and, consequently, no safety nets.

The use of an appropriate protocol provides the structure with which participants can give feedback in a way that protects the safety of the presenting teacher. With a little practice, protocols begin to change the culture to one where colleagues are *expected* to offer critical feedback and think deeply about the presenting teacher's work and be invested in it. Participants learn to separate the *work* from the *person* who has created the work. This last point is essential. When this separation becomes the culture, the PLC has made a marked growth spurt and the corollary improvements in teacher work contribute to more substantial student learning (McDonald, Mohr, Dichter, & McDonald, 2007).

Warm Feedback

As noted earlier, the *Tuning Protocol* includes segments specifically marked for giving warm and cool feedback (see Figure 3.1, Segment 6). The intent of warm feedback is not celebratory; it exists to identify specific pieces or characteristics of the work that are important for the presenting teacher to maintain. Warm feedback *is* affirming; these comments highlight the strengths in the work and aspects that the presenting teacher will want to keep in subsequent versions of the work. The more specific the warm feedback, the more useful are the comments made to the presenting teacher. General, sweeping comments rarely offer anything of practical value. Consider the examples in Figure 3.2.

Figure 3.2   Effective and Ineffective Warm Feedback

Examples of Effective Warm Feedback	Examples of Ineffective Warm Feedback
"The rubric is nicely aligned to the standard Ms. Begin is assessing."	"This is really good. I like it."
"The self-evaluation piece is good for students to force them to think about where they are in the process."	"I think the self-evaluation piece is a good idea."
"I like the way Ms. Breland has the kids start with the question, proceed to looking for solutions, and then to giving evidence in support of their solutions."	"This lesson is well-organized and packed with lots of goodies."

As illustrated in Figure 3.2, effective warm feedback is more than general praise. When it is specific, it is more validating and more useful to the presenting teacher. Note also that in the third example of effective warm feedback, the offering teacher uses the phrase *I like*. Prefacing warm feedback comments with *I like* is not ideal because it has an evaluative feel, but I have found that teachers say this quite naturally when offering warm feedback and it is not something for facilitators to strongly discourage. I tell my PLCs to try to state the feedback as an attribute of the work without *I like*, but not to worry if they slip up.

Cool Feedback

For many teachers, offering cool feedback is the hardest part of being a member in an effective PLC. Yet, despite its difficulty, it is absolutely essential for real growth. Teachers initially feel very uncomfortable offering cool feedback, even with effective structures in place for giving it. Teachers offering cool feedback often feel more angst with the feedback process than the teacher receiving the feedback. No matter, offering cool feedback is essential if we want our PLCs to grow and we want to authentically improve our teaching and the learning of our students. There's no getting around this. With just a little practice, though, giving cool feedback becomes as natural as giving warm feedback and the cool feedback tends to go deeper with every chance to engage in it. In time, presenting teachers who grow comfortable with the process begin to have high expectations for the cool feedback section of the protocols, as if to say, "Thanks for all the nice warm feedback, but tell me what I can do to make this work better."

If we try to remove ourselves, our teacher egos, from the process of giving and receiving feedback, we can be more objective in looking at the work. When cool feedback is given for the right reasons—to help the teacher receiving it—it will be heard in the right way. If cool feedback is given for the wrong reasons, for example, to feed the ego of the offering teacher, it will be obvious to the receiving teacher (as well as to the other participants) and it will be heard in that way. When our interests as givers of cool feedback are the interests of the presenting teacher, he is likely to appreciate our cool feedback. PLC coaches should impress upon group members that by *not* offering cool feedback, they are being *disrespectful* to the presenting teacher, as if to say that the teacher's work isn't important enough to think deeply about and offer suggestions for improvement. This is a seismic shift in thinking about feedback for most teachers. It is a shift that in many ways clinically defines an authentic PLC.

What typically happens during the cool feedback segment of the *Tuning Protocol* is that participants offer suggestions to help make the work better. This is a good thing. In fact, this is largely the interest of the teacher presenting work in the first place. (Interestingly, in the early days of the

Tuning Protocol, suggestions were discouraged. Feedback was limited to warm and cool only, with the thought that by offering cool feedback without suggestions, the presenting teacher would discover for herself the things to do to make the work better. We've learned a lot since then.) Though suggestions can really help the presenting teacher move the work forward, it should be stressed that it is perfectly okay to offer cool feedback without some accompanying suggestion to "fix" the perceived problem. Participants are not obligated to "fix" the issues that may be present in the work. Their only obligation is to point out the gaps and offer an idea if one comes to mind. If the cool feedback segment becomes a "suggestionfest," the presenting teacher quickly becomes overwhelmed with all the ideas, and the suggestions themselves tend to stray from what is practical and morph into lofty, unrealistic ideas with no practical merit. It is better to stay focused on what is there in the work and not get lost in the labyrinth of what might be idealistically possible.

Because it is generally easier to offer a suggestion than a criticism, teachers will gravitate to suggestions. Again, this is generally a good thing. One way to offer suggestions while giving cool feedback is for teachers to first state the gap or issue with the work and then offer the suggestion. For example, instead of saying

> *Maybe Ms. Gamblin could use the language of the State objective in her rubric,*

it is more informative to ground the suggestion in an observation by saying something like

> *Her rubric dimensions refer to skills that are different from the skills listed in the objective. It might help if Ms. Gamblin used the language of the State objective in her rubric.*

Positing the problem first and then following with a suggestion motivates the suggestion and is generally heard as more helpful. By going straight to the suggestion, there is an underlying message that *something* was problematic, but it may be unclear to the presenting teacher as to what it actually was. Examples of effective cool feedback with suggestions are listed in Figure 3.3.

It is essential to carefully consider the language used in the delivery of the cool feedback. This is not to suggest that we need to sugarcoat problems in the work. But some phrases shut the presenter down and, as a result, any valid points made fall on defensively deaf ears. A good rule of thumb is to avoid autobiographical suggestions. Teachers hearing feedback do not want to hear what *we* do, even if what we do is effective, and they may dismiss good ideas that start with phrases such as, "What I do is. . . ." Teachers giving feedback are tempted to say this, I have found,

Figure 3.3   Examples of Effective Cool Feedback With Suggestions

It seems to me that this assignment was too rushed for the kids. Maybe taking an extra day would be beneficial.

I think the text was too long for them to draw quality inferences. I think Ms. Whitley might try using shorter pieces of text to introduce them to inference and then give them longer text as they get better at it.

I don't see any higher order items on this assessment. I recommend one or two free-response items in which the students have the opportunity to apply these concepts to real-world scenarios.

because it is their way to establish credibility with the presenting teacher. Unfortunately, the presenting teacher often hears such comments as self-congratulating and overweening. A more effective delivery may begin with, "One thing Ms. Parrish might try is. . . ." This will be heard as helpful instead of boastful and, if the idea has merit, it will have credibility without the self-proclaimed credibility.

In addition to avoiding autobiographical suggestions declaring what we do, it is important to refrain from language that sounds attacking. Phrases like, "Why didn't she . . . ?" should be replaced with, "I'm wondering if she could have . . . ," and "I'm concerned about . . ." should be replaced with "One disconnect I see is. . . ."

Notice that in each of the aforementioned examples of useful cool feedback, the offering teacher (the teacher giving the feedback) refers to the presenting teacher (the teacher receiving the feedback) in the third person. This is deliberate. At some point in the evolution of the *Tuning Protocol,* coaches who facilitated the protocol noticed that when offering teachers gave feedback as if they were discussing the work among themselves, instead of giving feedback directly to the teacher whose work it was, the feedback was generally of higher quality. As such, offering teachers made good points about the work, points they were less inclined to make had they been speaking eyeball to eyeball with the presenting teacher. By speaking to the group as though the presenting teacher is not in attendance, the offering teachers feel the freedom and safety to say what they need to say. It's a bit awkward for PLCs the first time feedback is offered in this way—as if the presenting teacher is not in the room—but, having tried it both ways, I can attest to the notable difference in the quality of the feedback when the offering and presenting teachers are both insulated from the uneasiness of giving and receiving feedback.

Giving cool feedback takes practice. As teachers, we are simply not used to giving it. We are quick to pat each other on the back but slow to offer honest, constructive criticism. Even when teachers use protocols with built-in mechanisms and time periods for offering cool feedback, it can be persistently awkward to do so, until it becomes part of the culture of the PLC.

In my experience working with PLCs with regard to giving feedback, I have learned that, despite intuition to the contrary, it is generally harder for teachers to *give* cool feedback than it is for them to *hear* cool feedback. Ironically, the most frequent remark I have heard by the presenting teacher during the debriefing process of the protocol is that she would have liked a little more cool feedback. Indeed, cool feedback and the suggestions that often accompany them provide the traction with which the work can move forward.

Clarifying and Probing Questions

In protocols designed to explore teacher or student work, there is almost always a segment of the protocol in which participants are requested to ask clarifying questions after the presenter has contextualized his work. *Clarifying questions* are questions asked by participants for the benefit of those participants to obtain additional information from the presenter as it relates to the work. These questions tend to address the "what?" "how?" "where?" "when?" and "how long?" of the situation surrounding the work. Clarifying questions do not ask "why?" or "Do you think . . . ?" They are simple, factually based questions that can be answered in a sentence or two. It is helpful to think of clarifying questions as the kinds of questions that a journalist for the local newspaper might ask in getting the facts for a story. Judgments, opinions, and values are not present in these questions. Consider the examples shown in Figure 3.4.

In some protocols (e.g., the *Consultancy Protocol*), after clarifying questions have been asked and briefly answered, there is a segment in which participants ask *probing questions* of the presenting teacher. In these protocols, this is done in place of a cool feedback segment. Figure 3.5 outlines steps of the *Consultancy Protocol.*

Probing questions are questions that guide the presenting teacher to think more deeply about her issue or assignment in a way that may challenge her underlying beliefs and assumptions. They often get at the heart of the matter and may question the premise on which the assignment is

Figure 3.4 Examples of Clarifying Questions

"Did the students work on this assignment in class or just for homework?"

"Is this their first exposure to *inference?*

"Was the pretest multiple choice?"

"Was this assignment for those kids who failed the pretest or for everybody?"

"Were the results from your first block class comparable to the results from fourth block?"

"Are these vocabulary words posted on your Word Wall?"

Figure 3.5

Consultancy Protocol

The Consultancy Protocol was developed by Gene Thompson-Grove, Paula Evans, and Faith Dunne as part of the Coalition of Essential Schools' National Re:Learning Faculty Program, and further adapted and revised as part of the work of NSRF.

A consultancy is a structured process for helping an individual or a team think more expansively about a particular, concrete dilemma.

Time: Approximately 50 minutes

Roles:

   Presenter (whose work is being discussed by the group)

   Facilitator (who sometimes participates, depending on the size of the group)

   1. The presenter gives an overview of the dilemma with which s/he is struggling, and frames a question for the consultancy group to consider. The framing of this question, as well as the quality of the presenter's reflection on the dilemma being discussed, are key features of this protocol. If the presenter has brought student work, educator work, or other "artifacts," there is a pause here to silently examine the work/documents. The focus of the group's conversation is on the dilemma. (5–10 minutes).

   2. The Consultancy group asks clarifying questions of the presenter—that is, questions that have brief, factual answers. (5 minutes)

   3. The group asks probing questions of the presenter. These questions should be worked so that they help the presenter clarify and expand his/her thinking about the dilemma presented to the Consultancy group. The goal here is for the presenter to learn more about the question s/he framed or to do some analysis of the dilemma presented. The presenter may respond to the group's questions, but there is no discussion by the consultancy group of the presenter's responses. At the end of the 10 minutes, the facilitator asks the presenter to restate his/her question for the group. (10 minutes)

   4. The group talks with each other about the dilemma presented. (15 minutes)

      Possible questions to frame the discussion:

      What did we hear?

      What didn't we hear that we think might be relevant?

      What assumptions seem to be operating?

      What questions does the dilemma raise for us?

      What do we think about the dilemma?

      What might we do or try if faced with a similar dilemma? What have we done in similar situations?

   Members of the group sometimes suggest actions the presenter might consider taking. Most often, however, they work to define the issues more thoroughly and objectively. The presenter doesn't speak during this discussion, but instead listens and takes notes.

   5. The presenter reflects on what s/he heard and on what s/he is now thinking, sharing with the group anything that particularly resonated for him or her during any part of the Consultancy. (5 minutes)

   6. The facilitator leads a brief conversation about the group's observation of the Consultancy process. (5 minutes)

based. Contrary to clarifying questions, probing questions tend to address the "why?" and "what for?" in relation to the work and participants ask these questions for the benefit of the presenting teacher. Answers to these questions are typically more elaborate than answers to clarifying questions, and they prompt the presenter to reflect and respond more thoughtfully. One good probing question can cause an *Aha!* moment for the presenting teacher that will have a lasting impact which transcends the particular assignment or issue in question. Moreover, one good probing question can have a similar effect on the rest of the group as members think about their own teaching or assignments.

Probing questions, more so than clarifying questions, often spawn follow-up questions. For this reason, it is good practice for PLCs to pause slightly after the presenting teacher has answered a probing question, since the participant asking the question might have an important follow-up question (one that might lead to the *Aha!* moment). It is instructive to think of probing questions as being the kinds of questions that a *60 Minutes* reporter might ask during an interview in getting to the heart of the matter.

Consider the examples in Figure 3.6.

When asking probing questions, it is important take care not to disguise a directive (or even a suggestion) as a probing question. There is a tendency for teachers to inject their own values and beliefs and frame them as probing questions. Sometimes it is up to the coach to determine

Figure 3.6   Examples of Probing Questions

"If a student is successful on this assignment, what piece of the assignment best convinces you he or she has mastered the learning objectives?"

Possible follow-up question: "How could your rubric be weighted to reflect the importance of this component?"

"What in your mind is the cost/benefit of this assignment? In other words, do you feel that the amount of learning matches the days invested in this assignment?"

Possible follow-up question: "How might you determine pacing for this assignment within your larger unit?"

"What do you think is the relationship between those kids acting out and their ability to do the work successfully?"

Possible follow-up question: "For those kids, what kinds of things can you do to make them more confident in their ability to be successful?"

"This assessment is multiple choice. How can you tell what they know or don't know if they get an answer wrong?"

Possible follow-up question: "If we can't tell the guessers from the kids who knew something and made careless mistakes, does it make sense to include free response items and award partial credit? How might you structure that?"

which is which. The line is often blurry and it is the coach's responsibility to jump in when her instincts tell her that a particular question crosses that line. For purposes of illustration, consider the following directives, disguised as probing questions:

Should you have taken off for spelling errors on this assignment?

Would the data be better represented as bar graphs rather than as pie graphs?

Do you think the poster is weighted too heavily in the scoring rubric?

In all three examples, the questioner is really making a direct suggestion, concealed rather transparently as a question. Respectively, the questions are saying the following:

You *should* take off for spelling errors.

The data *would* be better represented with bar graphs.

The posters *are* counted too much in the rubric.

While all three suggestions may have sound educational merit, the point of probing questions is to encourage the presenter to think about these things in a manner that challenges the teacher's assumptions. The goal is that the presenter might come to his own conclusions about spelling expectations, graph choice, the disproportionate weight of assessment components, and so forth. With practice, participants learn how to *probe* rather than *direct* with their questions, coaches learn how to referee questions, and the presenting teacher comes to expect and appreciate his colleagues' questions to help his work improve. Don't expect the magic (as one principal with whom I have worked called it) to happen the first time.

BRINGING AND EXAMINING WORK

Teaching is a complex enterprise and the kinds of work a teacher might bring to the table for the PLC to examine and discuss are varied. Sometimes, a teacher (or team of teachers) may seek assistance with a unit plan or project. Other times, it may be an assessment about which the teacher wishes to receive feedback. Still other times, it may be a work in progress or an issue or dilemma the teacher is facing that is problematic. No matter the work, there is a commensurate protocol suited to assist the discussion to make the work better. As we see later in this chapter, choosing the best-suited protocol is important. Otherwise, the feedback can be flat or focused on the wrong things (see *Matching Work to Protocols*).

Teachers in authentic PLCs are in the habit of owning each other's problems. They have a prevailing attitude that "we're in this together" and that a problem owned by one teacher is a problem owned by the entire PLC. The spirit is one of unity and not one where competition and judgment reign. The presenting teacher is bearing her soul and the unspoken backdrop to the goings-on in authentic PLCs is, "What can we all do to solve this problem or make this work better?"

That said, it is essential for teachers to bring work—their own or that of their students—that is in need of input from the PLC. A common occurrence I have observed in PLCs beginning to share work is for presenting teachers to bring their best unit, their best project, or the assessment of which they are most proud. This stems from a tendency of presenting teachers to guard themselves against too much feedback. If presenting teachers bring their best work, their thinking goes, suggestions to improve it will be minimized and affirmations of the work and their teaching will be maximized. If and when this happens, these presenting teachers are taken aback and sometimes offended when the work they bring—good as it may be—is nonetheless offered cool feedback and suggestions for improvement. I advise PLCs who are early in the process of using protocols to avoid bringing their best work. It is better to be a bit vulnerable by bringing work that truly needs feedback than to bring their best material and be disappointed by the feedback. In this way, the work can really improve and the presenting teacher is not put off by the experience and comes to welcome the suggestions the PLC offers.

Framing Questions

Several protocols for examining teacher and student work request the presenting teacher to prepare and share a *framing question* when the initial context of the work is presented. Framing questions serve the purpose of focusing the team (and therefore the feedback) on that component of the work or issue about which the presenting teacher desires the most help. Figure 3.7 provides some sample framing questions.

During the segment of the protocol in which the presenting teacher provides the initial context for the work, she states her framing question. Members of the PLC make note of the question and coaches often record it on chart paper or on the whiteboard for all to see and refer back to during

Figure 3.7   Examples of Framing Questions

"For this assignment, are my plans to support my weaker students without neglecting the middle and high ability kids adequate? "

"What do you see in the student work samples that explains why the quality of work was so low?"

"Is there enough 'meat' to this project? What other components should I consider including to make the project more rigorous?"

the feedback phase. It is the job of the PLC coach to remind the team of the framing question in the event that the focus of the feedback discussion strays from the central area in which the presenter sought help.

Framing questions are generally effective for the purpose of keeping participants focused on the presenter's concern, but their company can be a double-edged sword. On the one hand, they help steer the team and honor the concern of a presenting teacher. On the other hand, they can limit the discussion to one specific attribute of the work that may not be the central cause of the problem but instead may be merely a symptom of a greater problem. For example, in the case of the second sample framing question in Figure 3.7, it may be that the low quality of the student work was due to insufficient scaffolding of the instruction that led to the work. This may not be evident in the work samples themselves (though it might be) but is only made clear from the context of the assignment given by the presenting teacher during the protocol. In this case, teachers offering feedback may see it suitable to discuss the instructional components and not the assignment or the work samples, per se. The presenting teacher is often so close to the work that her perception of the problem may not be the problem at all. If coaches are too militant in insisting that PLCs address only the issue embedded in the framing question, opportunities for offering useful feedback and encouraging new insights on the part of the presenter may be lost. So while framing questions can be useful, PLC coaches have to decide if and to what extent the team will be allowed to stray from the framing question, in the best interest of the presenting teacher, her work, and her students.

Matching Work to Protocols

As mentioned, some protocols for examining teacher and student work are better suited than others, depending on the work being presented. I recommend PLCs start with either the *Tuning Protocol* or the *Notice & Wonder Protocol*. The *Notice & Wonder Protocol* is outlined and explained in Chapter 5, since it is particularly well suited to looking at data (the subject of Chapter 5), but it can also be useful in examining student work. The *Notice & Wonder Protocol* is a good place for PLCs to start looking at work, and the advantage of this lies in the fact that there is no feedback segment, per se. Instead, PLCs make objective observations about the work in the first phase (the *Notice* phase), followed by a second phase, in which participants pose queries about the work (the *Wonder* phase).

The *Tuning Protocol* not only remains in my opinion the most useful tool for examining student and teacher work, but it is relatively easy for PLCs to use. Teachers are generally more comfortable offering warm and cool feedback—even in cases where the cool feedback primarily consists of suggestions—than in asking the probing questions that are required by other protocols, such as the *Consultancy* and *Charette*. As the PLC gains comfort with protocols in general and the *Tuning Protocol* in particular, and as they become a more united, trusting, and seasoned PLC, they can venture out to the *Consultancy Protocol* and *Charette Protocols*. There is no good reason to rush the process; in time, PLCs' comfort with protocols and their need to try new ones will naturally dictate their readiness to use the *Consultancy Protocol* and the *Charette Protocol* and others listed in the Protocols and Activities Appendix to support important discussions about teaching and learning. The steps to the *Charette Protocol* are outlined in Figure 3.8.

Figure 3.8

Charette Protocol

Original written by Kathy Juarez, Piner High School, Santa Rosa, California.
Revised by Gene Thompson-Grove, January 2003, NSRF.
Revised by Kim Feicke, October 2007, NSRF.

The following list of steps attempts to formalize the process for others interested in using it.

1. A team or an individual requests a charette when
   a. the team/individual is experiencing difficulty with the work,
   b. a stopping point has been reached, or
   c. additional minds (thinkers new to the work) could help move it forward.

2. A group, ranging in size from three to six people, is formed to look at the work. A moderator/facilitator is designated from the newly formed group. It is the moderator's job to observe the charette, record information that is being created, ask questions along the way, and occasionally summarize the discussion.

3. The requesting team/individual presents its "work in progress" while the group listens. (There are no strict time limits, but this usually takes 5 or 10 minutes.) Sometimes, the invited group needs to ask two or three clarifying questions before moving on to step 4.

4. The requesting team/individual states what it needs or wants from the charette, thereby accepting responsibility for focusing the discussion. The focus is usually made in the form of a specific request, but it can be as generic as "How can we make this better?" or "What is our next step?"

5. The invited group then discusses while the requesting team/individual listens and takes notes. There are no hard and fast rules here. Occasionally (but not usually) the requesting team/individual joins in the discussion process. The emphasis is on improving the work, which now belongs to the entire group. The atmosphere is one of "we're in this together," and our single purpose is "to make a good thing even better."

6. When the requesting team/individual knows it has gotten what it needs from the invited group, they stop the process, briefly summarize what was gained, thank the participants and moderator, and return to the "drawing board."

7. Debrief the process as a group.

Figure 3.9 provides a general summary of the types of work for which the three common protocols are suited.

Figure 3.9   Three Common Protocols

Tuning Protocol
> Teacher-produced work
> Student-produced work

Consultancy Protocol
> Issues and dilemmas related to teacher-produced work
> Issues and dilemmas resulting from student-produced work

Charette Protocol
> Teacher work still in the planning stages that has hit a "dead end"—an obstacle or problem that has prevented the work from moving forward to completion

Figure 3.10 details the kinds of teacher and student work that may be considered for examination.

Figure 3.10   Examples of Teacher and Student Work

Teacher-Produced Work

Assessment-Related Work
> Ungraded tests or quizzes
> Portfolio requirements
> Student projects
> Writing assignments
> Rubrics
> Computer-based assessments
> Lab reports

Instruction-Related Work
> Individual lessons (including technology-based lessons)
> Unit lessons
> Plans for lesson warm-ups
> Plans for lesson closure
> Instructional activities (including games)
> Plans for intervention
> Computer-based instruction

Classroom Procedures
> Homework policies
> Grading policies

Procedures for grouping students

Discipline policies

Time management

Student-Produced Work

Graded Assessments

Tests or quizzes

Student portfolios

Student projects

Student writing samples

Lab reports

Research papers

Computer-based assessments

Classwork Assignments

Homework Assignments

Nearly every aspect of teacher work, from plans for a detailed unit project to a simple idea about a classroom policy, can be accommodated by one of these three protocols. There are many other protocols; some useful ones are outlined in *The Power of Protocols* (McDonald et al., 2007). For a more comprehensive (and slightly overwhelming) list of protocol possibilities, the NSRF and SRI (School Reform Initiative) websites are encyclopedic resources (http://www.nsrfharmony.org/protocol/protocols.html and http://school reforminitiative.org/protocol/).

A word of caution regarding the use of protocols is in order. A thorough discussion of feedback (warm, cool, probing questions) should precede any attempt to first use protocols. Failure to do so may, at best, result in an experience that is void of anything but superficial feedback; at worst, it may precipitate a violation of trust and safety that may leave PLC members with a lasting "bad taste" about protocols. If this happens, it is hard to go back and "do one right," much harder than it is to do it well the first time. When PLC coaches front-load the experience with a thoughtful discussion addressing the roles and types of feedback and the initial awkwardness that is common with the formality of the process, they reap the worthy dividends of a well-executed protocol. PLC members must be on the same page about what to expect, how protocols work, and why segments of the protocol are in place to ensure safe, quality discourse about their work. Like anything new, the initial awkwardness will fade, and as protocols are conducted under the careful eye of a good coach, they soon become the preferred modus operandi by PLC members.

In the final section of this chapter addressing the examination of student and teacher work, I turn to one of the most important but least traveled avenues for looking at teacher work: observing teachers in the act of teaching.

PEER OBSERVATIONS

Purpose and Potential

In the early 1980s, as a third-year teacher, I was asked to teach math in a rigorous summer program at one of the nation's leading private schools in Connecticut. There, I was struck by many things, not the least of which was the prevalence of visits by colleagues to my classroom. Nary a day went by in which someone wasn't observing my teaching. It was not because I was a beginning teacher; every faculty member could have made the same claim. It was because of the school's culture, established long before my arrival to the beautiful New England campus. Teachers there routinely observed one another. It was a professional obligation to observe and a professional expectation to be observed. I learned a great deal from that experience, both as observer and as the one being observed.

Peer observations are an avenue for looking at teacher work, and they are also one of the hardest things for schools to fully embrace. Yet they are one thing that can skyrocket the collective level of team unity and the individual learning curves of the teachers who comprise the team. At their least, they provide teachers with firsthand knowledge of what their colleagues do in the classroom; at their best, they afford teachers the opportunity to learn from each other in a way that cannot be realized by teacher talk at even the most productive PLC meetings. If PLCs are to truly break down the walls of teacher isolation, they must step out of the meeting room and into each other's classrooms.

Plausibility of Peer Observations

The most compelling reason for the fact that peer observations are not widespread in many schools is one of time and scheduling. In most schools with which I work, there is simply no time for teachers to observe one another. Teachers have one coveted planning period each day and the demands of team planning, department meetings, and PLC meetings prohibit them from getting their own work done (correcting papers, planning individual lessons, etc.) let alone observing a colleague. In most cases, neither the teachers themselves nor their administrators have placed peer observation terribly high on crowded priority lists. To be sure, even administrators often relegate their own observations of their faculties low on their lists and many have all they can do to make their rather obligatory annual rounds of visits to classrooms. The absence of peer observations in our schools today may well be the last bastion of teacher isolation that permeates even the most collaborative school cultures.

For schools that prioritize peer observation as a viable means toward team unity and individual teacher growth, there are ways to make this happen. The least disruptive way to do so is to hire a "floating substitute" who is assigned to cover classes of different teachers during different periods throughout the school day. For each class "freed up" by the substitute, a classroom teacher can observe two colleagues, each for a half of a period. In two days' time, on a four-by-four schedule, 8 teachers can observe 16 classes. If this were to happen on a monthly basis throughout the school year, 80 teachers can observe 160 classes. That means, for example, each eight-member PLC from five different departments can observe 32 classes, with each individual member observing four colleagues, all the while being absent from her own classroom only twice throughout the school year. After a single school year, the culture of peer observation would be fairly well established among the faculty and this last wall of isolation would start to crumble. The *Fusion Model* for teacher professional development, developed at Osmond Elementary School in Lincoln County, Wyoming, is centered on teachers observing and learning from other teachers. The model is implemented with on-staff, full-time substitutes whose job it is each day to cover classes of observing teachers (Semadeni, 2010).

After visits have taken place, it can be the focus of scheduled PLC meeting times to use protocols to discuss the observations, so that each observation is a learning experience for the observer and the observed, as well as for the entire PLC. It is essential that the mindset be that both the observer and the observed can gain valuable insights during peer observations and that the presupposition is not one of evaluation or judgment on the part of the observing teacher.

A second option for overcoming the time and scheduling constraints that often accompany the prospect of peer observation is for PLCs to use their regular PLC meeting time for observations. For these meetings, PLC members scatter throughout the building and each observe two teachers. Since in grades 6–12 PLCs are most often configured by subjects, this option assumes that teachers will be unable to observe teachers in their own PLC and instead visit classroom teachers outside their subject areas. While there may be content gaps for the observer, it has been my personal experience that this nonetheless proves to be very enlightening for the observer (and somewhat less nerve-racking for the teacher observed). The multitude of student-teacher interactions that occur in a single period (or half a period) transcends subject matter content in most instances. It tends not to matter that an algebra teacher is observing (quite possibly some of her same) students as they struggle to interpret and understand the Bill of Rights in a social studies class. And there can be prearranged reciprocation, at which time the social studies teachers observe the math classrooms.

As a third option, in some faculties with whom I have worked, we elected to videotape classroom teachers and then use the excerpts of the footage in a PLC *Tuning Protocol* or *Notice & Wonder Protocol* to offer feedback and share insights from having viewed the class. This requires a high level of trust in the PLC and by the classroom teacher whose class will be examined. While this technique can be significantly beneficial for the whole PLC, it may be ill-advised for PLCs not yet ready to open up in this way. Teachers are generally not comfortable with the camera, at least initially, and its presence can sometimes make for disingenuous responses on the part of students. PLCs can also view classroom footage from National Board Certified Teachers (NBCTs) on staff who were required to videotape a lesson as part of the NBCT application process. Videotaping teachers is no substitute for having the eyes and ears of a colleague present during the lesson, but it has the potential to provide important discourse about teaching and learning at subsequent PLC meetings.

If peer observation is a priority for PLCs and their administrators, there are ways to make it a painless, productive reality for faculties. The aspects of good teaching—and even not so good teaching—can be witnessed, discussed, and improved by experiencing inter- or intra-PLC peer observations. No matter which option is pursued, peer observations stand to add an essential ingredient to looking at teacher work toward the goal of examining our practice and improving the quality and quantity of our students' learning.

SUMMARY: LOOKING AT WORK

Looking at student and teacher work, the first of the three Essential Tasks, is a central pursuit of authentic PLCs. Without carefully looking at what we do and what our students produce, we are not likely to significantly improve our instruction. Critical conversation about our work is seldom easy, in large part due to a prevailing teacher culture in many schools that has not been conducive to open and honest dialogue in this realm. Authentic PLCs are in the habit of constantly bringing work to the table and looking to the power and effectiveness of using carefully matched protocols to assist in these important conversations. Protocols foster useful and substantive feedback, which is at the heart of looking at work.

As PLCs gain experience by using protocols to examine student and teacher work, their initial uneasiness with the structure and formality of the protocols is assuaged. As this happens, PLCs grow comfortable with the process and they soon look for suitable protocols in discussing a broad range of issues relating the teaching and learning.

Peer observations provide a kind of "real-time" look at teacher and student work and can greatly accelerate the growth of the PLC and of the individual teachers who comprise it. There are creative ways to schedule these and, in schools whose principals make this a priority, peer observations stand to raise faculty trust and collaboration to new heights. In such schools, the notion of being a collaborative team transcends individual PLCs and soon encompasses a culture in which the entire faculty is a team and acts as a PLC in its own right.

In the next chapter, we examine one prominent type of teacher work: teacher-designed formative assessments.

4

Designing Quality Common Formative Assessments

One-shot professional development workshops, exciting new programs pitched by zealous publishers, and the latest technotools from SMART Technologies all have their places in promoting better instruction. They are, however, no match for the benefits realized from having teams of teachers design quality formative assessments that they will administer to their students. Few things dictate instruction more significantly than teachers' knowledge of exactly how their kids will be assessed at the end of the instructional unit. Disbelievers in this notion need only look at how instruction has markedly changed since NCLB legislation in 2001. Teachers respond most dramatically when they know at the onset of instruction the content of the test to be given at the end. They tend to "teach to the test," whether those tests are summative state EOC tests or team-designed unit tests. This is not inherently bad; if the tests to which the teachers are teaching adequately assess the desired learning outcomes, then teaching in a manner that prepares the students to demonstrate mastery on these tests is largely the point of instruction. If the assessments are of high quality and written at the onset of instruction, the instruction that leads to them is often of equal high quality. If, on the other hand, the assessments are of lesser quality, so too is the preceding instruction likely to be.

As schools across the nation adopt schedules that permit common planning, the writing of common assessments is becoming part and parcel for what teacher teams do during their common planning periods. Designing common formative assessments (CFAs) marks the second of the three *Essential Tasks of Authentic PLCs* mentioned in Chapter 1. CFAs provide important data to PLCs in assessing the effectiveness of classroom instruction. They are, among other things, a significant source of *ongoing* data.

In a nutshell, CFAs are assessments—most commonly, tests—that all members of the PLC write collaboratively for the purpose of finding out what kids know and are able to do so that teachers can appraise their teaching and adjust instruction in accord with that appraisal. For example, a unit test on plot, character development, and catharsis written and administered by the Language Arts PLC provides valuable information about not only what kids know, but also about how well teachers in the PLC have taught the material, as well as what they need to do next, instructionally, so that all kids learn.

This chapter explores writing quality CFAs and provides the backdrop for Chapter 5 (looking into other valuable sources of data and developing plans to put the data to good use in informing and altering instruction).

DECIDING ASSESSMENT CONTENT

Before PLCs can adequately design CFAs that align with state standards, they must first be very clear on what that content is and what is most important to emphasize, and they must be thoroughly familiar with their state curricula.

Revisiting Essential Learning Outcomes

In Chapter 2, under the heading *Constructing Community Knowledge,* I discussed criteria for PLCs to use in deciding Essential Learning Outcomes (ELOs). Those criteria were *prominence* and *vitality.* Recall that a learning outcome has *prominence* if it is weighted heavily on the state assessment and it has *vitality* if mastery of the learning outcome is necessary for later work. By proceeding as prescribed in Chapter 2, PLCs can use these criteria to decide which topics or subgoals from state curricula should be emphasized and which should be de-emphasized or eliminated completely. PLCs must make these important decisions prior to writing assessments. That is, they must decide what they will teach and what they will not teach. Surprisingly, despite the obviousness of that last statement, it is too often the case that teachers never really discuss ELOs.

Unpacking the Standards

If deciding ELOs addresses the "what to teach," unpacking the standards gets at the degree of depth and complexity with which students are to master the elected learning outcomes. A useful approach to unpacking the standards is for PLCs to go through the written state standards and place each substandard into one of two categories: *Outcomes students must know or understand* and *Outcomes students must be able to do.* Once all of the substandards are separated by category, PLCs have the task of dissecting the wording of each substandard. PLCs do this by identifying the action verbs of each substandard and noting the degree of complexity implied by the verbs. Many PLCs find it helpful to analyze the action verbs in the context of Bloom's Taxonomy (or the increasingly popular *Revised Bloom's Taxonomy*).

To clarify this process of unpacking the standards, consider the following example (see Figure 4.1) using Goal 4 from the North Carolina Standard Course of Study for Math 7. For illustration purposes only, let us suppose that a Math 7 PLC has used the rubric outlined in Chapter 2 and scored the prominence and vitality of each substandard listed in Goal 4. Indicated in lined-out text are those substandards that the PLC decided were low on the prominence-vitality scale.

After the ELOs have been extracted from all of the substandards listed under Goal 4 (the substandards are indicated by text that is not lined out), the PLC separates these ELOs into two categories: *Outcomes requiring students to know or understand concepts* and *Outcomes requiring students to be able to perform skills.* For our hypothetical Math 7 PLC, Goal 4 substandards might be separated as follows (see Figure 4.2).

It is noteworthy to observe that the nonessential substandards (indicated in lined-out text in Figure 4.1) have been removed from the *Know/Be Able to Do* chart in Figure 4.2. If the PLC decides that these substandards

Figure 4.1   North Carolina Standard Course of Study for Math 7 Goal 4

COMPETENCY GOAL 4: The learner will understand and use graphs and data analysis.

Objectives

4.01   ~~Collect~~, organize, analyze, and display data (including box plots and histograms) to solve problems.

4.02   Calculate, use, and interpret the mean, median, mode, range, ~~frequency distribution, and inter-quartile range~~ for a set of data.

4.03   Describe how the mean, median, mode, range, ~~frequency distribution, and inter-quartile range~~ of a set of data affect its graph.

4.04   Identify the outliers and determine their effect on the mean, median, mode, and range of a set of data.

4.05   Solve problems involving two ~~or more~~ sets of data using appropriate statistical measures.

Source: North Carolina Department of Public Instruction (strikethrough added), 2003

Figure 4.2   Know/Be Able to Do Chart for Math 7 Goal 4

Know or Understand	Be Able to Do
• Interpret the mean, median, mode, and range for a set of data. • Describe how the mean, median, mode, and range of a set of data affect its graph. • Determine how outliers effect the mean, median, mode, and range of a set of data.	• Organize, analyze, and display data (including box plots and histograms) to solve problems. • Calculate and use the mean, median, mode, and range for a set of data. • Identify the outliers of a set of data. • Solve problems involving two sets of data using appropriate statistical measures.

do not pass the *prominence-vitality* test, there is no need to explore them further. The job of the PLC is to focus only on the ELOs.

Also note that some substandards, for example 4.02, are divided into partial substandards and occupy dual positions in the *Know/Be Able to Do* chart. Namely, in the case of 4.02, *calculating* and *using* the mean, median, mode, and range fall into the category of performing a skill to be mastered by students; *interpreting* what these statistical measures denote is more a matter of *understanding* what these measures are than it is a skill to be performed. This is a bit tricky since *interpreting* is, after all, something one does; yet the underlying implication of *interpreting* is that students *understand* the meaning of the statistical measures. PLCs must take pains to discuss the essence of each substandard so as to not misappropriate their placement in the *Know/Be Able to Do* chart based solely on the verb.

Once the substandards are carefully placed in the *Know/Be Able to Do* chart, PLCs identify the action verbs in each and come to some agreement about the degree of complexity required by the substandard. Many schools are using the Revised Bloom's Taxonomy written by Lorin Anderson and David Krathwohl in 2001. In ascending levels of complexity, the Cognitive Process Dimensions are as follows (Anderson & Krathwohl, 2001):

1. Remembering

2. Understanding

3. Applying

4. Analyzing

5. Evaluating

6. Creating

Again, let's suppose our Math 7 PLC classified the substandards North Carolina Goal 1 using the Revised Bloom's Taxonomy and arrived at the following (see Figure 4.3):

Figure 4.3   Levels of Complexity for Math 7 Goal 4

Know or Understand	Degree of Complexity Based on Anderson's and Krathwohl's (2001) Revised Bloom's Taxonomy
• *Interpret* the mean, median, mode, and range for a set of data.	2. Understanding
• *Describe* how the mean, median, mode, and range of a set of data affect its graph.	2. Understanding
• *Determine* how outliers affect the mean, median, mode, and range of a set of data.	4. Analyzing
Be Able to Do	Degree of Complexity Based on Anderson's and Krathwohl's (2001) Revised Bloom's Taxonomy
• *Organize, analyze*, and *display* data (including box plots and histograms) to solve problems.	5. Evaluating 4. Analyzing 3. Applying
• *Calculate* and *use* the mean, median, mode, and range for a set of data.	1. Remembering 3. Applying
• *Identify* the outliers of a set of data.	1. Remembering
• *Solve* problems involving two sets of data using appropriate statistical measures.	3. Applying

By establishing ELOs from the list of state standards and by unpacking the content of each substandard, the teachers have a clear sense of what they will teach and to what degree of complexity they will teach it. They have, at this juncture, decided assessment content. The next question for them becomes this: *How will we test mastery of this content?*

In order to optimize impact on student achievement, it is necessary for test-writing PLCs to shake loose old paradigms of test design and abide by three critical shifts in thinking with regard to the following:

1. Designing Standards-Based Assessments

2. Scoring Assessments and Assigning Grades

3. Reviewing CFA Data and Planning for Intervention

DESIGNING STANDARDS-BASED ASSESSMENTS

Aligning tests to the ELOs is critical. This bedrock alignment must reflect both content (the what) and degree of complexity (the rigor) of the state standards. In my experience in working with schools on their teacher-designed assessments, the former is more easily achieved than the latter. Teacher teams are generally adept at assessing the content and have more difficulty assessing the degree to which students truly understand the concepts. Assessing the degree of student understanding of complex ideas presupposes that teachers include higher order items on assessments that are compatible to the degree of complexity they identified as they unpacked the standards. Their assessments must require students to explain their reasoning, synthesize various kinds of information, and apply rote facts and knowledge. When assessments demand these of students, teaching to the test becomes an appropriate and useful pursuit, something that we *should* be doing.

When collaborative teams of teachers in a PLC write tests that are *standards-based* in both content and degree and are designed to determine where students are along the journey of mastery of these standards, the tests begin to look different from textbook-driven tests and serve a purpose other than to merely put grades on kids.

Standards-Driven Versus Textbook-Driven Assessments

Standards-based tests focus on specific, state-mandated learning objectives and stray from the usual practice of testing chapter contents. When student mastery of a specific standard becomes the teachers' preeminent goal, teachers write tests to measure students' degrees of mastery instead of measuring the incidentals typically included in textbook chapter contents. The same textbooks are used in many states, yet each state has its own version of the standards for the particular course in which the textbook is used. And while textbook publishers aim to provide content that is as generic as possible and therefore usable by many different states, publishers often write textbooks with the big clients in mind (for example, New York, Texas, and California). It goes without saying that the content of such books may not completely align with the standards of the multitude of states who would adopt the book. As such, individual topics may be underemphasized or overemphasized for any particular state when it comes to curricular alignment.[1]

When teachers write tests that are standards-driven, tests become standards-aligned and not merely minirepresentations of what the textbook publishers thought important. For example, instead of a math test covering sections 3.1 to 3.5 from the book, a standards-based test would assess students' mastery of a particular standard, say, *Using Equations of Lines to Model Real-World Applications*. Similarly, a paper written in English class should not assess students' knowledge of Mark Twain but rather assess their mastery of a language arts standard regarding plot, character development, imagery, symbolism, and so on. When we shake out the

---

1. As noted earlier, as the Common Core State Standards take hold in states across the nation, I suspect this tendency will change as textbooks are written to align with the Common Core State Standards.

standard to be learned and separate it from the vehicle used to master the standard, we focus more on the end (student success on the state assessments) and not the means (student success on the textbook content).

The Problem With Textbook Tests

In my work with PLCs and schools, I have witnessed a common practice of teachers and departments using textbook chapter tests as their CFAs. There are several problems with this.

First, chapter tests included at the end of the textbook chapter on a particular topic reflect the emphasis of what the textbook publisher thought important and thereby may not align with the state or Common Core standards. These textbook tests may do a good job assessing the chapter contents—though this is sometimes debatable—but if the textbook contents fail to align fully with state or Common Core standards, then the tests won't either, by default.

Second, when teachers use the textbook chapter tests, they focus their instruction on teaching to the textbook; again, this causes them to assign a back seat to the actual state standards in favor of a dependence on what the textbook publishers deemed important, whether or not those emphases align with state or Common Core standards. This encourages an instructional focus on the textbook instead of one on the state or Common Core standards.

Third, chapter tests included in most textbooks typically shoot low on Bloom's Taxonomy in terms of rigor, assessing only a broad and basic understanding of the topics at hand. As such, these tests often fall short in requiring the degree of complexity that state EOCs require. When student success on textbook tests is the goal, students are very often ill-prepared to succeed on state assessments.

In essence, when teachers use textbook chapter tests as their CFAs, they not only risk failing at assessing all appropriate content, they also risk assessing the appropriate content at a level that may not be commensurate with the state EOC assessments that their students face at the conclusion of the course. For these reasons, I urge PLCs to design their own CFAs that align more closely with state or Common Core standards both in terms of what they're testing and how rigorously they're testing important concepts.

The Problem With Multiple-Choice Tests

Standards-based formative assessments tend to include fewer, if any, multiple-choice items. Despite the ease with which teachers can score multiple-choice items (and the allure of such convenience), multiple-choice tests provide little useful information about what individual students know and are able to do. For example, if a student gets a multiple-choice question wrong, how can we know whether the student knew nothing about the content of the question and simply guessed or whether the student knew something about the content of the question but did not know enough to select the correct response? This becomes especially problematic in cases where the multiple-choice question itself tests several skills at once, a common feature of multiple-choice items in subjects like math. If a student gets the question wrong, where was the breakdown in the student's knowledge or understanding? We just can't tell.

The counterpoint I often hear from teachers who favor multiple-choice tests is that such tests mimic the format of the state tests their students will face at the end of the year. Therefore, the argument goes, students should be exposed to this format often throughout the year. While all EOC state tests do contain mostly—if not exclusively—multiple-choice items, it is important to keep in mind that these tests are summative in nature. CFAs, by definition, are designed to be *informative.* That is, CFAs serve to provide important information about what students know and what they do not know. Except for providing very general information about a class as a whole, multiple-choice tests fall short in providing the kind of information that teachers need to know about what kids have and have not mastered, both individually and collectively. Unless and until teachers have this kind of information about their students' learning, they are incapable of acknowledging and responding appropriately to student learning gaps.

Planning Backwards

Teachers write standards-based tests before instruction ever begins. When they do so, all instruction that precedes the assessment is expressly targeted to the goal of having students perform successfully on the assessment. Writing assessments before instruction begins and gearing all instruction to promote student success on that assessment is analogous to the football coach designing every team practice to arm his players with the skills they need to beat their city rival on Friday night.

Starting with the end in mind and then proceeding with instruction to accomplish that end is commonsensical and not a terribly new idea. (Indeed, traditional tests—not just standards-based tests—can have this particular attribute.) Grant Wiggins has been urging this for decades and was the first educator I heard use the term "planning backwards" (which for some reason in many circles is now called "backwards planning") when he was Senior Researcher for the CES in the late 1980s. He and Jay McTighe have since offered many useful strategies and insights in their work, *Understanding by Design* (Wiggins & McTighe, 2004). Teachers internalize this idea of writing assessments first fairly quickly and can transition to writing tests before instruction begins without too much retooling. This is fortunate, as doing so in and of itself raises the instructional bar. When teachers write their assessments at the conclusion of instruction, there is a commonplace tendency for them to write tests on the basis of what their students can successfully do at that point in time rather than writing them based on the degree of complexity that the state or Common Core standards require.

Formative Use of Tests

I formally discern between formative and summative assessments when we explore data in Chapter 5, but I believe it helpful to touch on the notion of formative assessment here as it is germane to CFAs.

Teachers must think of their assessments as ways to inform them on the job they're doing. Formative assessments are not assessments whose primary function is to put grades on kids, although the reality and hindrance of having to assign grades continue to lurk in the foreground. (I address grading in some detail later in this chapter.) Summative assessments, such as final exams or state EOCs, exist primarily to serve this function. Formative assessments, by definition, exist to find out what our students have learned and how well we have succeeded in teaching them. That goes without saying that tests can no longer be isolated, final measures of student mastery; instead, they must be catalysts for *what happens next* in terms of our instruction. When teachers write tests to assess *both* student mastery *and* teacher effectiveness, tests inform educators about what to do with students who miss the mark and fail to demonstrate mastery. Postassessment intervention becomes a natural by-product of formative test results, and deciding on an appropriate plan for intervention becomes one important job of the PLC.

Standards-Based Assessments at a Glance

Figure 4.4 highlights some important characteristics we have discussed thus far of standards-based tests as they compare to customary tests.

Figure 4.4 Customary Versus Standards-Based Assessments

Standards-Based Assessments	Customary Tests/Assessments
Assessment *for* instruction	Assessment *of* instruction
Standards-driven (content and organization)	Textbook-driven (content and organization)
Part of the fabric of instruction (ongoing)	Culminates instruction (finite)
Written before instruction begins	Written after instruction takes place
Multiple grades, one for each standard assessed	Single grade across multiple standards
Built-in provision for addressing nonmastery, reevaluation	No provision for reevaluation
Many constructed response items	Many multiple-choice items
High on Bloom's Taxonomy	Low on Bloom's Taxonomy

ALTERNATIVE FORMS OF COMMON ASSESSMENTS

Far and away, most of the formal assessing that teachers conduct happens in the way of tests, quizzes, or something in between I call quests. As we'll see in Chapter 5 in a treatise on data, there are many other sources of formative information that teachers use—much of it on a daily basis—that help them gauge how their students are progressing in mastering ELOs. When it comes time to assess students formally, however, most often teachers do so by administering written tests. That said, I would be remiss if I neglected to discuss the place of assessments alternative to written tests.

Alternative assessments such as student projects, presentations, and portfolios can provide teachers with important information about how well their students have learned the essential outcomes. The added benefit of alternative assessments is that they tend to cast a broader net in terms of allowing for individual student learning styles. Student projects, presentations, and portfolios give students who typically don't perform well on written tests the chance to demonstrate their mastery in different, frequently more creative ways. As such, alternate means to traditional written assessments of student mastery often get at the heart of the purpose of assessment: to find out what kids know and are able to do. This goal supercedes the narrowly focused goal of simply getting kids to do well on tests.

But in order for student projects, presentations, and portfolios to be meaningful in assessing student mastery, they must be well designed and abide by the following:

- Alternative forms of assessment should be rigorous and content-rich.
- Alternative forms of assessment should align to the ELOs (not merely assess other related skills and concepts).
- Alternative forms of assessment should be evaluated with a standards-based rubric.

Standards-Based Rubrics for Alternative Assessments

One of the problems with alternative forms of assessment in assessing student mastery is that student projects, presentations, and portfolios very often lack substantive subject content. When these types of assessments are poorly designed and stripped of the wonderfully creative elements that students may have produced—the flashy posters, so to speak—teachers are many times left with the nagging question, "But what did the students actually learn from having completed this assignment?" The problem is usually not that the project, presentation, or portfolio *couldn't* have been content-rich, but more that the project, presentation, or portfolio simply *wasn't* content-rich. In these cases where students have complied with the requirements set forth by the teacher to produce "stuff," the students have not necessarily demonstrated subject content learning.

A way around this dilemma is for teachers to evaluate alternative assessments using a standards-based rubric instead of the commonplace "checklist rubric" that tends to demonstrate merely *what* was produced. Checklist rubrics—if you can call them "rubrics" at all—typically list the component parts of an alternative assessment (e.g., paper, poster, presentation) that students *perform* in completing the assessment. Teachers then "check off" that students have completed the various aspects, generally without regard to levels of quality. If students *do* the poster, they get up to 10 points; if they *submit* a paper, they earn up to 20 points; and if they *do* a presentation, they may be awarded up to 15 points.

Standards-based rubrics evaluate the *learning* that is evident in the components of the work and not simply the presence or quality of the *components* themselves. This notion suggests a significant shift in how teachers write rubrics for alternative assessments. To put it simply, it's not what the student *did* that matters; it's what the student *learned* from having done it that matters. The driving question should be this: *Where in what the student did is there evidence of learning?* Consider the following example to illustrate this essential difference.

Suppose that an Algebra 1 ELO is for students to find, interpret, and predict information from a line of best fit for two related sets of data. Let's also suppose that the Algebra 1 PLC has decided to assess their students' mastery of the above ELO by assigning students a project they're calling *Scatterplotting Sports.* In this project, pairs of students are to examine data from a sports-related website of their choosing (e.g., www.nba.com).

The PLC sets forth the following requirements for the project. Student pairs will

- Choose two sets of related data, either from individual players or teams (e.g., free-throw percentages and points scored for games in a season)
- Construct a poster-sized scatterplot of their data
- Find the equation of the line of best fit
- Interpret the meaning of the slope and intercept of their line
- Use their line to make a prediction
- Present their findings to the class

This project is an example of a worthy alternative assessment that is of general interest to students and aligns nicely to the state standard requiring students to be able to find and interpret a line of best fit and predict information from the line (Bullets 3, 4, and 5 in the previous list). The other ancillary tasks of choosing data, constructing a poster, and presenting the findings to the class are all meaningful skills required by the project, but those skills are not required by the state standard. Therefore, it is essential that teachers write a rubric that reflects a lesser weight of these required but nonessential components of the project.

All too often, when teachers assign projects like *Scatterplotting Sports,* they write rubrics that place too much emphasis on the "stuff" that students produce, like posters and presentations, and not enough emphasis on the demonstration of learning goals (finding and interpreting a line of best fit and predicting information from the line). Standards-based rubrics emphasize the demonstration (or not) of student mastery of the ELOs. Though there is nothing wrong with students producing amazing posters followed by dazzling presentations, these components are not the fundamental purpose of assigning the project and the rubric should reflect the relative unimportance of these in contrast to students demonstrating that they can indeed find and interpret a line of best fit and predict information from the line. A standards-based rubric for the *Scatterplotting Sports* project might look as shown in Figure 4.5.

The rubric in Figure 4.5 acknowledges that students produced a poster and made a presentation to the class, and it provides a measure of evaluation for those tasks. As teachers know all too well, there are those students who would not bother to make the poster or presentation if they were not receiving a grade of sorts for their efforts. So it is fitting to include dimensions reflecting those tasks in the rubric. After all, we want students to do a good job on the tangibles we're asking them to produce. However, when teachers write rubrics with weighted dimensions, as in Figure 4.5, they can control the scoring emphasis to be on what's most important—mastery of the state learning objectives—and not on the vehicle students use to show evidence of their mastery (the poster and the presentation).

SCORING AND GRADING CFAs

Obsolescence of Customary Grades

For over 100 years—as far back as I can tell from researching the history of grading students—American schools have in some form or another used the grades of A, B, C, D, and F to categorize student achievement. These designations have for many of these years served a useful purpose in grading students, both on individual assessments and in assigning marking period and year-end grades to students. These grades have historically provided a practical measure of discerning how much and how well a student has learned the required content in any particular course. To be sure, most school districts across this nation continue to use these same grades on everything from class work, to homework, to quizzes and tests, and to marking period and year-end grades for students.

The problem with these designations is that, in a new age characterized by meeting state standards, these age-old grades have outlived their usefulness. It is no longer useful for teachers to separate students into

Figure 4.5 Rubric for *Scatterplotting Sports* Project

Rubric Dimension	Weight	3	2	1	0	Points Earned
Proficiency in finding *Line of Best Fit*	× 3	Equation for the *Line of Best Fit* is accurate and written with proper mathematical notation.	Equation for the *Line of Best Fit* is accurate; there are minor mistakes with mathematical notation.	Equation for the *Line of Best Fit* is inaccurate.	Equation for the *Line of Best Fit* is not indicated.	
Proficiency in interpreting *Line of Best Fit*	× 3	Significance of slope and y-intercept is accurately and completely explained in the context of the data.	Significance of slope and y-intercept is accurately interpreted in the context of the data.	Significance of slope and y-intercept is partially explained in the context of the data; some misunderstandings are present.	Slope and y-intercept are found but not explained in the context of the data, or they are interpreted inaccurately.	
Proficiency in applying *Line of Best Fit* to make predictions	× 3	Accurate predictions and comparisons are made using the *Line of Best Fit*; student understands the real-world significance of predictions individually and collectively.	Accurate and sensible predictions are made using the *Line of Best Fit*; student understands the significance of predictions in context.	Accurate predictions are made using the *Line of Best Fit*; student shows partial understanding of the significance of predictions in context; minor errors may be present.	Predictions are made using the *Line of Best Fit*; student fails to understand the significance of predictions in context, OR no predictions were made using the *Line of Best Fit*, OR inaccurate predictions were made.	

(Continued)

Figure 4.5 (Continued)

Rubric Dimension	Weight	3	2	1	0	Points Earned
Choice of data	×1	Data sets have meaningful, real-world connections and are insightful and interesting to explore.	Data sets are appropriately connected and sufficient in number.	Data sets are somewhat connected but lack meaningful, real-world application.	Choice of data shows a lack of understanding regarding scatterplots and the relationship among different quantitative data.	
Scatterplot poster	×2	Information is well-organized, accurate, complete, easy to read, and colorful; graph is clearly labeled; pictures or graphics are included.	Information is well-organized, accurate, complete, and easy to read; graph is clearly labeled.	Information is organized and accurate; there are minor omissions in content; graph is labeled.	Information is disorganized; errors or omissions in content are present; graph is partially labeled.	
Presentation	×2	Information is thorough, accurate, and clearly explained; students are engaging and poised; visual enhancements are used effectively; questions are answered well; both students contribute equally.	Information is thorough, accurate, and clearly explained; visual enhancements are used effectively; most questions are answered well; both students contribute equally.	Information is accurate, though minor points are neglected; visual enhancements are used; questions are answered with some uncertainty; both students do not contribute equally.	Information is incomplete or inaccurate; visual aids are not used effectively or at all; questions are poorly answered; one student does most of the presenting.	

categories, distinguishing between students by letter grades, because the issue is no longer one of determining where students are along a graduated scale of mastery. The new issue in the post-NCLB era has become essentially binary in nature: *Has the student mastered the required learning objectives?* And if he has not, the corollary question (rarely entertained in the old paradigm) becomes this: *What will we do so that he does (master the learning objectives)?* There is no middle ground.

When we boil grading down to these critical questions, everything that a PLC does focuses on student success, rather than on who earned a B or who earned a C on our assessments.

In the end, there is no continuum of mastery. Students either demonstrate mastery on a particular substandard or they fail to do so. Though I propose in the next section four grading categories into which students may fall in their mastery, these categories are based on mastery (or not) of specific and individual learning objectives. The customary continuum of A–F never served to measure mastery or partial mastery of individual learning objectives; it has always represented *overall* grades—usually decided by percentages—of student performance on assessments that measured multiple learning objectives. As such, these customary grades delineated how much of the whole students had learned, with no regard for how students did on the individual standards that made up the whole.

A by-product of using the outdated A–F grading scale has been the practice of using percentages to decide these customary designations. Students answering 95%–100% of the test items correctly, for example, earn a grade of A. Students answering 85%–94% of the items correctly get a B, and so on. Again, this grading schema discerns levels of mastery insofar as it designates what percentage of the learning objectives were mastered by a student, but it makes no attempt to separate students into the only two categories that matter: students who have mastered the individual objectives and students who have not.

As educators operating in the post-NCLB world of state assessments, we must step back from the pre-NCLB paradigm of assigning students grades based on a percentage of mastery and move to a new paradigm of acknowledging that some students have mastered a particular learning objective and that others have not yet done so. When teachers think this way, in terms of mastery and nonmastery instead of in terms of percentage-mastery, they begin to see the limitations of the antiquated A–F grading scale.

It would be naïve to think schools can completely dismiss the reality of having to assign customary grades to students. School districts and school boards will continue to expect teachers to use these grades for recording marking period and year-end grades. But what if teachers and PLCs used a different scale along the way for individual teacher-designed assessments, such as a scale more consistent with identifying mastery and nonmastery? If we must, we can always convert the new, more descriptive designations to the customary grades for marking period and year end grades (and I make suggestions for doing so later), but for the CFAs PLCs are designing, let's consider using a different scale, one more pointedly focused on mastery.

Standards-Based Test Grades

When teachers design standards-based tests as prescribed earlier, tests that assess fewer objectives with each objective carrying its own grade designation, grades on those assessments change accordingly. If the purpose of testing is to gauge student mastery against a set of standards, the customary grades of A, B, C, D, and F become riddled with the limitations mentioned. A new system of grading begins to have more meaning, one that reflects mastery or nonmastery *per learning objective*. For *each* learning objective that is assessed on any single assessment, I suggest the following alternative grading scheme (see Figure 4.6):

Figure 4.6   Suggested Mastery Level Designations

Grade Designation	Meaning	Classification	Description
MH	Mastery with Honors	Mastery	Exceeded minimum requirement for mastery; virtually no mistakes or omissions
M	Mastery	Mastery	Met minimum requirement for mastery; minor mistakes or omissions; evidence of some understanding
PM	Partial Mastery	Nonmastery	Failed to meet minimum requirement for mastery; "fixable" mistakes or omissions; minor intervention required before reassessment
I	Intervention	Nonmastery	Failed to meet minimum requirement for mastery; major mistakes or omissions; major intervention required before reassessment

It is worth noting that grade designations in Figure 4.6 are greater in number than merely *mastered* and *not mastered*. The four grade designations I suggest function so that the teacher can demarcate those students who excel in demonstrating mastery of the learning objective (MH), from those students just meeting the standard (M), from those students who know something but still need some work before successfully mastering the material (PM), and from those students for whom serious instructional intervention is necessary (I). But in the end, students have either mastered the standard (MH, M) or they have not (PM, I). For this reason, students earning a designation of PM or I have more work to do and they will require future reassessment against the standard.

It is important to stress that these designations of MH, M, PM, and I do not equate to the customary grades of A, B, C, D, respectively. These new designations are not grades in the usual sense; they are designations regarding where a student is in terms of her mastery of a specific standard after an assessment of a learning objective has been given and scored. The PLC that has written the assessment gets to decide what constitutes a MH, M, PM, or I. Whether the PLC defines these designations based on point values or percentages or some other measure is immaterial. The point is that the PLC decides where the bar is for each designation for each learning objective and that students performing at or above the bar (for M) are designated as demonstrating mastery and those performing below the bar (for M) are not, at least not yet. Customary designations can still be assigned at some point (and they are usually required), but those will be determined by benchmark requirements set by the PLC. We can convert these new designations into cumulative marking period grades of A, B, C, D, and F—and we do so later— but for now, it is essential to assess student mastery based on mastery against a particular standard. MH, M, PM, and I are used only to reflect where any given student is against a standard or substandard in a *particular point in time.* This is a fundamental and critical shift in thinking for most teachers.

So long as teachers assess student performance on each learning objective with its own grade designation, an argument could be made for continuing to use the customary designations A–F for these individual grade designations. The PLC would still need to decide the criteria used to make such designations (see *Criteria for Mastery,* next section). However, in working with schools on establishing grade designations and deciding whether to stick with the customary A–F labels, I have observed that, even when PLCs assign separate grades for each learning objective, those PLCs who cling to the A–F designation tend to revert back to a traditional *percentage mentality* that obscures the purpose of standards-based grading. For this reason—though I admit it is a significant shift for teachers—I suggest PLCs break free of A–F grading (at least until marking period grades are due) and try these new designations.

As teachers move away from grades as labels and toward grades for discerning mastery of individual standards, all grades become more informative and less categorizing. Grades begin to tell teachers less about who did well and who did not and more about what needs to happen with regard to individual learning objectives. This ensures that all students are learning and demonstrating mastery of the required standards.

Criteria for Mastery

Teacher teams who have written and administered CFAs to their students must decide together how those assessments will be scored. PLCs must come to consensus about what constitutes mastery (MH, M) for each objective being tested, as well as what constitutes partial and nonmastery (PM, I). This is most often done with a team-written rubric or by assigning point values to the various components that are required by the test items.

It may seem foreboding for PLCs to write rubrics or partial credit point scales for each objective on each assessment, but it is often the case that the rubrics or point scales, once written, are generic enough to be recycled and applied to future assessments covering new content. For example, consider the following partial credit rubric for scoring free-response items on secondary math assessments (see Figure 4.7). This rubric assumes that all tested items are worth a maximum of 3 points.

Figure 4.7   Partial Credit Rubric for Secondary Math Items

Points Earned	Approach	Procedure	Answer
3	Valid	No errors	Correct
2	Valid	Minor errors or omissions	Incorrect
1	Valid	Major errors or omissions	Incorrect
0	Invalid or missing	NA	NA

This rubric can be used for a variety of free-response test items in math, independent of the particular content being tested. It can be used relatively quickly; if a student answers an item correctly and the student's approach to the item is valid, she is awarded the full 3 points. If she answered the item incorrectly, then the teacher must decide if the errors present are minor (e.g., sign errors) or major errors or omissions and award either 1 or 2 points based on that determination. Math teachers with whom I have shared this rubric particularly like the fact that students who answer a question without accompanying work are not awarded points for the item. When students are informed of the rubric beforehand, they quickly learn that they must show their work to receive any credit on the test item. (Getting students to show their work is an age-old battle fought by many math teachers.)

Using this model, each item on a math assessment is a 3-point problem. Students answer each question and teachers award them 0, 1, 2, or 3 points based on the *Partial Credit Rubric* in Figure 4.7. Since there are likely to be several questions measuring student mastery of any particular substandard on the CFA, the Math PLC must decide how many total points the student must earn in order to receive each of the possible designations of MH, M, PM, and I for that particular substandard.

To illustrate this, let's suppose a 10-item math CFA assesses mastery on two related substandards. Information about the complexity level for each item as well as the breakdown for Criteria for Mastery for both substandards might be as follows (see Figure 4.8):

Figure 4.8   Sample Criteria for Mastery

Criteria for Mastery: Substandard A	
CFA Item	Maximum Points Possible
Question #1 (low complexity, assesses basic knowledge that was explicitly taught)	3
Question #2 (low complexity, assesses basic knowledge that was explicitly taught)	3
Question #3 (low complexity, assesses basic knowledge that was explicitly taught)	3
Question #4 (moderate complexity, assesses basic and intermediate knowledge)	3
Question #5 (high complexity, assesses application of basic and intermediate knowledge)	3
Question #6 (high complexity, assesses application of basic and intermediate knowledge)	3
Total Points Possible for Substandard A	18
Minimum Points for MH Designation	17
Minimum Points for M Designation	14
Minimum Points for PM Designation	9
Point Range for I Designation	0–8
Criteria for Mastery: Substandard B	
CFA Item	Maximum Points Possible
Question #7 (low complexity, assesses basic knowledge that was explicitly taught)	3
Question #8 (moderate complexity, assesses basic and intermediate knowledge)	3
Question #9 (moderate complexity, assesses basic and intermediate knowledge)	3
Question #10 (high complexity, assesses application of basic and intermediate knowledge)	3
Total Points Possible for Substandard B	12
Minimum Points for MH Designation	11
Minimum Points for M Designation	10
Minimum Points for PM Designation	7
Point Range for I Designation	0–6

A few observations are notable. First, in order for a student to receive a mastery designation of M for either substandard, he must earn at least partial credit on the most complex problems, in addition to earning full credit (3 points) on the less difficult problems. Of course, in the case of substandard A, any combination of 14 points will earn him a designation of M. The PLC decides what skills or knowledge students must minimally demonstrate to earn a mastery designation. The point is that, in our example, the student cannot merely answer correctly the easy and medium difficulty problems and earn enough points for a designation of M. He must have *some* success—even if only in part—with the most challenging items. This notion of having students demonstrate at least partial knowledge of the most challenging items is what Spence Rogers refers to as *Mastery Lock* (Rogers, 2009). This practice of Mastery Lock guarantees that no student earns a designation of M on any particular substandard by only answering successfully easy or medium difficulty items. Teachers can be comfortable with a reasonably high standard for designating mastery as long as they afford subsequent opportunities for students to demonstrate mastery. This is discussed more fully in later sections of this chapter.

A second observation to note is that there is no need for teachers to assign an overall designation on the CFA. In fact, this would be hard to do. Since each substandard carries its own Criteria for Mastery, it only makes sense that these mastery designations remain independent. Though the substandards may have related content, mastery on one may or may not impact the likelihood of mastery on another. Convincing teachers to abandon the usual practice of assigning overall grades on assessments covering multiple learning objectives is not easy, but it is a necessary paradigm shift in how teachers track student mastery of individual substandards.

For our *Scatterplotting Sports* project, once teachers evaluate the various components of the project using the rubric in Figure 4.5, they need to decide where the bar is for students to earn a designation of mastery on the substandard. Since the rubric was point-based, the Algebra 1 PLC might decide on the following point scale for designations of MH, M, PM, and I (see Figure 4.9):

Figure 4.9   Sample Criteria for Mastery for Scatterplotting Sports Project

Mastery Designation	Criteria for Mastery
MH	Total points earned > 37 points
M	Total points earned: 28–37 points
PM	Total points earned: 20–27 points
I	Total points earned < 20 points

In the same way we used Mastery Lock on the test items in Figure 4.8, we can also use it on the *Scatterplotting Sports* project. Notice that for students to earn a Mastery designation, they must earn the equivalent of 2 points for each dimension in the rubric. In reading down the rubric in the "2-point" column in Figure 4.5, it seems appropriate that students who perform as described in that column of the rubric be considered as having mastered the substandard. This is a deviation from the usual *percentage mentality*; if we divide the points earned by the total possible points (42), a student awarded 28 total points on the project would receive a 67%—a failing grade in most schools! PLCs decide where the bar is for mastery and devise scales for these grade designations.

In the same way a math PLC can decide rubrics for discerning levels of mastery on individual test items and also for the Criteria for Mastery of a particular substandard being measured on the assessment, so too can teachers and PLCs of other subjects. English language arts teachers can have generic rubrics for writing essays or research papers. Science folks can do likewise for scoring lab reports and so forth. The point is to have a team-decided barometer for what constitutes mastery (and partial mastery).

Scoring Calibration

Once PLCs write CFAs and rubrics for Criteria for Mastery for each substandard assessed on the CFA, I advise teachers in subject-specific PLCs to swap student papers with each other the first few times they give CFAs. That is, each teacher in the PLC scores the student work of a colleague. Since the assessment was written by the PLC and the scoring rubric was as well, teachers ought to be able to score papers from students they do not teach but who have been taught by a colleague and presumably have mastered the same material. By doing so, members of the PLC achieve a sort of *scoring calibration*. When teachers score each other's papers, they are more apt to score papers without regard to the common sentiments of "It's good work for him" or "She tried so hard on this" and other distracters from measuring student work based on mutual, predetermined standards of mastery.

The Grade Book

Most traditional chapter or unit tests are usually quite long, require most of the class period to administer, and cover many different standards or objectives. The end result generally finds teachers entering a single grade into the grade book. This is the most compelling bit of evidence that grades have been traditionally used to put labels on kids rather than to keep track of their mastery of specific learning outcomes. For example, a grade of B– entered into the grade book next to a student's name on a

Chapter 3 Algebra test covering linear functions tells us almost no information about which concepts and skills the student learned regarding linear functions in comparison to the skills about which she learned little or nothing. Without the corrected test in hand, the teacher would likely be incapable of using the grade book alone to tell a parent what the student knows and does not know about linear functions. (Yet, teachers cling to such grade books at every parent meeting, as if they actually told us information other than "Derrick got a B– on the Linear Functions test.") This age-old paradigm of entering one grade on assessments that span multiple learning objectives is fundamentally flawed.

Instead, tests should be smaller both in terms of the number of test items and the number of learning objectives being tested. They should assess mastery of one to three learning objectives/standards. I've started calling these *quests*—larger than traditional quizzes but smaller than traditional tests. (The name also serves to remind us that the purpose of these assessments is for teachers to gain information about how their students are progressing toward mastery of a standard (or a few standards) and how teachers are doing in moving students toward mastery. That is, after all, the *quest*.)

Second, except for alternative forms of assessments that are graded holistically with a rubric, teachers must adopt a practice of assigning a separate grade designation (for example, MH, M, PM, I) to each standard being tested on the assessment. Therefore, except in cases where teachers are testing only a single substandard or in cases of alternative assessments, there is no need for an overall grade on the quest.

And third, for those assessments that do measure mastery of several substandards, teachers must begin to enter a grade designation for each substandard being assessed. For example, if a quest assesses mastery of three learning objectives, then teachers record three separate grade designations for that one assessment. A grade book organized this way, with separate columns delineating grades for each substandard being measured, reveals valuable information regarding how each student is progressing through the required standards. This move from composite grades to disaggregated grades is a critical characteristic of standards-based grading and assessing. The sample grade book page in Figure 4.10 shows how teachers might keep track of student mastery of a CFA assessing one to three substandards.

Assigning Marking Period Grades

When the time comes to assign traditional grades of A, B, C, D, and F for quarter, semester, or year-end grades, I recommend that the PLC decide these traditional designations based on the number of standards a student has mastered (i.e., the ones for which a student has received

Figure 4.10   Sample Grade Book Page of Student Mastery

Student Name:	Substandard:				Substandard:				Substandard:			
	MH	M	PM	I	MH	M	PM	I	MH	M	PM	I
1.	○	○	○	○	○	○	○	○	○	○	○	○
2.	○	○	○	○	○	○	○	○	○	○	○	○
3.	○	○	○	○	○	○	○	○	○	○	○	○
4.	○	○	○	○	○	○	○	○	○	○	○	○
5.	○	○	○	○	○	○	○	○	○	○	○	○
6.	○	○	○	○	○	○	○	○	○	○	○	○
7.	○	○	○	○	○	○	○	○	○	○	○	○
8.	○	○	○	○	○	○	○	○	○	○	○	○
9.	○	○	○	○	○	○	○	○	○	○	○	○
10.	○	○	○	○	○	○	○	○	○	○	○	○
11.	○	○	○	○	○	○	○	○	○	○	○	○
12.	○	○	○	○	○	○	○	○	○	○	○	○
13.	○	○	○	○	○	○	○	○	○	○	○	○
14.	○	○	○	○	○	○	○	○	○	○	○	○
15.	○	○	○	○	○	○	○	○	○	○	○	○
16.	○	○	○	○	○	○	○	○	○	○	○	○
17.	○	○	○	○	○	○	○	○	○	○	○	○
18.	○	○	○	○	○	○	○	○	○	○	○	○
19.	○	○	○	○	○	○	○	○	○	○	○	○
20.	○	○	○	○	○	○	○	○	○	○	○	○
21.	○	○	○	○	○	○	○	○	○	○	○	○
22.	○	○	○	○	○	○	○	○	○	○	○	○
23.	○	○	○	○	○	○	○	○	○	○	○	○
24.	○	○	○	○	○	○	○	○	○	○	○	○
25.	○	○	○	○	○	○	○	○	○	○	○	○
26.	○	○	○	○	○	○	○	○	○	○	○	○

a designation of M or MH). For example and purposes of illustration only, the team may decide that, of the 20 substandards taught and assessed in a particular marking period, traditional grades might be assigned as follows:

A = 18–20 standards mastered (received designations of MH or M only)

B = 15–17 standards mastered

C = 12–14 standards mastered

D = 10 or 11 standards mastered

F = fewer than 10 standards mastered

It is not necessary or desirable for PLCs to use traditional percentages in determining how they will match the number of assessments mastered with a corresponding traditional grade. Depending on the content and the importance of individual standards, it may be the case that a smaller percentage of mastered standards constitutes a B, for example. As with the Criteria for Mastery, PLCs would be well advised to abandon *percentage mentality* and the usual percentage scales and decide these ranges based on the work itself.

Having to put traditional grades on kids at some point does not mean that we are done trying to move them to mastery of as yet unmastered material. It is just that the reality of assigning grades cannot be ignored. Again, it is the decision of the PLC how customary letter grades will be awarded. PLC team members are uniquely qualified to decide grading scales for their students.

REVIEWING CFA DATA AND PLANNING FOR INTERVENTION

Reviewing CFA Data

Once PLC teams have written and given CFAs and decided how those assessments should be scored, it is essential that they review the results of these assessments. This happens first by the individual teachers who score and review the results of their classes. After that, team members come together and review their collective results. This is not so much to compare the effectiveness of individual teachers but to come to some agreement about what to do with those students who have not demonstrated mastery and determine what to do next to ensure that these students acquire the necessary skills in the areas in which they are lacking. This collective reviewing of the CFA data is critical in moving all students toward the goal of mastery of the standards.

Planning for Intervention

For the first decade of my teaching career, I was that math teacher who gave tests based on the chapters in the textbook, graded them, passed them back to kids, and moved on to the next chapter. I didn't give the students review days before tests and I didn't generally give them retests (unless the entire class did poorly). I resented teachers who gave retests; they spoiled and spoon-fed kids, I contended, and those teachers tacitly sent the message that students didn't have to study much the first time around since a retest waited in the wings. If a portion of my class did poorly, I told them to study harder and that they'd see the material again on the final exam in May. Plenty of kids did fine on the test, I argued; therefore, I must have done a fine job teaching it. After all, I would insist, they all received the same instruction. (In 1990, no one I knew was talking about *differentiated instruction*.)

Well, I will go on record maintaining my continued distaste for review days, but I have changed my mind about retests. If we are really focused on moving kids toward mastery of specific standards, we must allow them multiple attempts to demonstrate mastery. And though they may all get the instruction at the same *time*, they don't all learn along the same *timeline*. If we really want all kids to learn at high levels and we want to hold them to rigorous standards of quality, then we have to make allowances for differences in how and when our students learn.

This is the essence of the increasingly common practice of differentiated instruction: Kids don't all learn in the same way and when they do, it is rarely at the same time. Teachers who have begun to recognize this fact and have adopted the practices of differentiating their instruction are now teaching in ways that yield more success for more students the first time those students are exposed to new material. This is key. The better the initial instruction, the fewer the number of students needing intervention. Carol Ann Tomlinson, arguably the most respected author and speaker on the topic of differentiated instruction, has written the following:

> Acknowledging that students learn at different speeds and that they differ widely in their ability to think abstractly or understand complex ideas is like acknowledging that students at any age aren't all the same height: It is not a statement of worth, but of reality. (Tomlinson, 2001, p. viii)

To accommodate their growing awareness of this reality, teachers have embraced and implemented the practices suggested by Tomlinson and other authors on the subject of differentiated instruction. But what happens when, despite our best efforts to differentiate our instruction, some kids still don't learn? What do we do with those students, whose learning styles we have so intently tried to accommodate, who nonetheless fail to demonstrate mastery on our assessments?

When we organize assessments around a few specific substandards, it starts to make more sense to provide students with multiple opportunities to demonstrate mastery. These opportunities take various forms. It tends not to matter if we actually give students a second test covering the material or if we reassess their mastery using some other modality (e.g., papers, projects, presentations, etc.). This is up to the PLC team to decide, and in so deciding, the team can factor in issues of fairness, practicality, scoring schemes, and such. Team members can also decide the bearing that the new assessment will have on the grade of the student. Issues like whether the new score will replace the old one or simply be averaged in with the previous score can and should be decided by the PLC (preferably before any instruction begins). On this note, I offer the following parallel, real-life standards-based assessment.

When my wife insisted that we sell her 2004 Saturn Ion and buy a scooter to reduce both our gasoline costs and our collective carbon footprint on the environment, the state required us to obtain motorcycle licenses. (I should mention that this was not one of those little 50cc scooters folks with suspended licenses drive; this was a 125cc scooter, necessitating the operator to have a motorcycle license.) And so we read the motorcycle handbook, went to the DMV, and took the written test. In North Carolina, we could get a maximum of five questions wrong and still pass the test. Of course, she got a perfect score and I got five wrong. This experience started me thinking about assessment and retests. Had I missed a sixth question, I would have failed the test, and I would have to return to the DMV at a later date after studying the book a bit more and try again. That is, I would be permitted to retest until I demonstrated mastery. And the final passing score, no matter how many attempts were required, would be my only score kept on my DMV record. The DMV doesn't average the scores. They consider only the latest score, the one in which mastery was achieved. Averaging multiple scores would have seemed silly.

Applying this principle to educational assessments, it seems fitting that we consider only scores from students in which they demonstrate mastery and not average the scores of all attempts leading to mastery. After all, we are interested in students demonstrating mastery and it seems to me inappropriate to use the common practice of weighing nonmastery scores in with the mastery score when deciding overall grades. But this is up to the PLC; if members decide that old scores will be included and that all attempts at mastery will be considered in the final grade for the assignment, then so be it. Like all things in the PLC realm, it is the responsibility of the PLC to engage in discussions about these things and make a determination with which members are most comfortable.

In addition to providing multiple opportunities for students to demonstrate mastery, there must be some provision for intervention that occurs between the opportunities. For me, had I failed the motorcycle test, intervention would have been restudying the handbook (or getting tutored by my wife). For students, it might mean obtaining afterschool help, visiting in-school learning labs, getting outside tutoring, doing in-class test corrections, and so forth. The school's daily schedule is an important factor in determining which interventions are feasible. PLC members, given the local restraints and scheduling parameters, must decide together what, how, and when the intervention will happen.

Response to Intervention

Response to Intervention (RTI), like the practice of differentiating instruction, is a practice that has become popular in many schools in recent years. RTI espouses a three-tiered approach to intervention so that all students master the ELOs. The tiers are commonly organized in a pyramid depicting all students receiving the core instruction at the base of the pyramid and with intervention efforts intensifying, with fewer numbers of affected students, as the pyramid tapers to the top. Figure 4.11 illustrates the intervention process using the three-tiered pyramid.

According to the National Association of State Directors of Special Education (NASDSE), as the intervention intensity increases from Tier 1 to Tier 2 to Tier 3, the number of students involved in the intervention decreases from 80% to 15% to 5%, respectively (NASDSE, 2006). To learn more about RTI and what kinds of interventions are appropriate and recommended for students in these tiers, I suggest *Pyramid Response to*

Figure 4.11   Three-Tiered Model for RTI

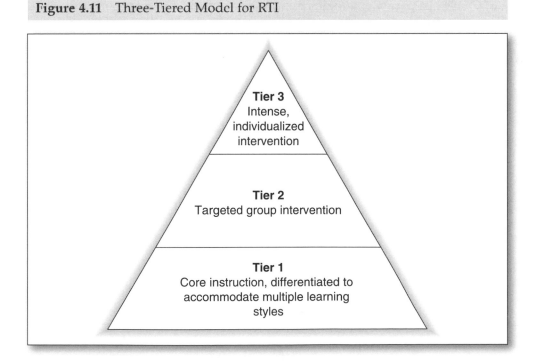

Intervention: RTI, Professional Learning Communities, and How to Respond When Kids Don't Learn (Buffum, Mattos, & Weber, 2009).

For our purposes here, it is enough to stress that PLCs must make provisions for when students don't learn, despite our best efforts to accommodate all learners by differentiating our instruction. The cycle of instruction, assessment, intervention, and additional assessment is essential for PLCs to reach their goal of mastery for all students.

SUMMARY: CFAs

In this chapter, we have discussed the second PLC Essential Task, designing quality common formative assessments. Some key points to keep in mind in designing CFAs are as follows:

- Quality CFAs are based on the state or Common Core standards, not the course textbook, and they can only be designed after PLCs decide ELOs for their students and unpack the standards and substandards.
- Quality CFAs are written by the PLC before instruction of the content begins.
- Quality CFAs contain few, if any, multiple-choice items.
- Partial credit for free-response items is decided by using a team-written scoring rubric.
- Quality CFAs assess one to three learning objectives (substandards), and a separate grade designation is awarded for each objective.
- Grade designations are based on a team-designed set of Criteria for Mastery, not on customary letter grades.
- Grade books are organized by learning objectives, not by sections in the textbook.
- Rubrics for alternative assessments are driven by evidence of learning, not by the tasks students complete.
- Plans for intervention are implemented for students failing to meet the minimum Criteria for Mastery.
- Students receive multiple opportunities to demonstrate mastery if they fail to meet the minimum Criteria for Mastery.

5

Reviewing and
Responding to Data

I n the last two chapters, we discussed the first and second Essential Tasks: *Looking at Student and Teacher Work* and *Designing Quality CFAs*. To be sure, both of these endeavors in and of themselves provide valuable sources of data. In this chapter, we examine how to look at other, more traditional sources of data, how to ask the right questions from the data, and what to do in response to these data so that the quality and quantity of student learning is increased. In many ways, this Essential Task holds the greatest impact as it allows teachers to first connect and then modify what they do to what students are learning. I begin with an overview of data in a general sense and proceed to explore how to use it in the classroom.

DATA LITERACY

Formative and Summative Data

NCLB legislation, and the surge of both state and local standardized assessments that followed, has made the educational community more keenly aware of the existence of both formative and summative types of data. While this is generally a positive thing, it has created a kind of perpetual confusion about the differences between these two types of data. In offering some clarity about formative and summative data, the primary criterion in deciding that one type of data is summative and another is formative is not so much in the data themselves but in *how the data are used*.

Data that are used to inform and alter instruction *along the way* toward student mastery are formative data. That is, formative data are used to *inform* teachers about how kids are learning, which then translates into modifications the teachers make in their instruction. In his work, *Transformative Assessment*, Popham offers a succinct and practical definition:

> Formative assessment is a planned process in which teachers or students use assessment-based evidence to adjust what they're currently doing. (Popham, 2008)

On the other hand, data that are used primarily to put labels on students (A, B, proficient, etc.), that serve to sort students into categories and are gathered after instruction has concluded, are summative data. With this type of data, there is no intention to use the data to alter instruction—at least not for the students to whom the data belong.

Rick Stiggins, author of the award-winning book *Student-Involved Classroom Assessment*, offers a clever distinction to help the matter: Assessment *for* learning is formative and assessment *of* learning is summative (Stiggins, 2001). Formative data are used to assist instruction—particularly in informing modifications to current instruction—while summative data assess the learning that has already taken place with no regard for how that learning could be improved while it is in progress.

Another oft-used analogy that aids in distinguishing between the two types is one involving medicine. Formative data is to blood work from an annual physical exam as summative data is to blood work from an autopsy. The first informs the patient in a way that can bring about changes in diet or lifestyle while the second provides information after the fact, without the possibility of modification to diet or lifestyle.

There is a prevalent misconception that EOC data is the only brand of summative data and that data gleaned from other sources such as teacher-designed classroom assessments are *prima facie* formative in nature. But when teachers give quizzes to students midway in a unit of study for the purpose of simply putting grades in the grade book without making use of that data in modifying subsequent instruction, the quiz results act as summative data. If, on the other hand, teachers use the same quiz results to differentiate instruction and offer additional support to students who performed poorly, the quiz results are used in a formative way. It all depends on how teachers use (or don't use) the data.

Even EOC data, typically summative in nature, can to some extent be used formatively as when teachers identify learning gaps and precipitate modifications to previous lesson plans for future cadres of students. While this is still largely after the fact, it can nonetheless impact important instructional changes.

Sources of Data

Effective PLCs are in constant pursuit of data. This is not because teachers are generally enamored with graphs and tables of numbers, but because they realize that, fundamentally, nearly everything a teacher does in and out of the classroom produces student data about how her students are learning. This information is often conspicuous, as in the case of EOC results or student performance on team-designed CFAs.

But it is essential to bear in mind that good data hide in the details as well. Every question a teacher asks her students during a lesson, every student response to those questions, every warm-up problem a teacher gives at the onset of a class period, every moment a teacher spends assisting individual students in a group setting, provides the teacher with valuable information about how her students are progressing in their mastery of a learning objective.

Teachers generally understand this and they process these data on a subconscious level. That is, teachers routinely respond to the data without tables and graphs of numbers and make alterations in their instruction to accommodate the information they glean constantly from their students.

Figure 5.1 highlights some possible sources of data, both the conspicuous, or *macrodata,* and the inconspicuous, or *microdata.*

Figure 5.1 illustrates the abundance of informal data available to teachers on a daily basis. Therein lies the secret of teachers who are in the habit

Figure 5.1   Examples of Macrodata and Microdata

Sources of Macrodata	Sources of Microdata
• Student scores on EOC Assessments • Student scores on Common Formative Assessments • Student scores on Projects • Student scores on District Assessments • Student scores on SATs, PSATs, Achievement Tests • Student scores on AP Exams • Student scores on DIBELS Tests • Student scores on Subject Placement Exams • Student scores on Computer-Based Modules • Student scores on Unit Pretests	• Student performance on quests • Student responses to teacher questions during lessons • Student questions during lessons • Student performance on warm-up questions • Student responses to *ticket-out-the-door* questions • Student performance during guided practice • Student performance during group work • Student performance during independent practice • Student performance on homework assignments • Student responses of CFUs (*Checks for Understanding*) • Student explanations at the board • Student posters • Student notebooks • Student portfolios • Student reflections in journals • Student performance on writing assignments

of using data formatively, to inform their instruction. They capitalize on the microdata—the daily data—in assessing constantly how their students are doing. When teachers neglect the microdata in favor of the macrodata, they unwittingly dismiss valuable information that can inform them of what they should be doing differently or additionally, so that all kids learn.

REVIEWING EXISTING DATA

In this age of state assessments, electronic grade books and attendance records, student demographic reports, IEPs, PEPs, SATs, APs, online surveys, web-based assessments, computer-based learning software, district quarterly assessments, and other local data sources, teachers and school leaders are bombarded by data. DuFour, DuFour, Eaker, and Many (2006) said schools are "data rich and information poor" (p. 215). The amount and variety of state-provided assessment data alone is sufficient to paralyze the average educator into a numbing state of inaction. Teachers have neither the time nor the expertise required to plunge into this numerical abyss. And so what tends to happen is that teachers only cursorily review data, often at a single department meeting. Sometime in August, teachers typically pass around EOC data which reflect the performance of last year's students, at which time teachers look at the tables of numbers and conclude that they need to spend X additional days on topic Y; everyone agrees and the data are, quite literally, never reviewed again.

Since so much of the data that classroom teachers ever see are summative in nature and "after the fact," the data arrive too late to change instruction for the students to whom the data belong. Even disaggregated data from state assessments are very general in nature: Our black students performed with less proficiency than our white kids; our students with disabilities have the fewest numbers of kids scoring on grade level; our girls outperformed our boys, and so on. While PLCs ought not overlook those generalities or discard them as unimportant, they don't exactly explain what is happening. *That* kids on free and reduced lunch scored worse than kids with more economic advantages does not tell us *why* they did so or *what* we might do differently to close the gap. For that, teachers and PLCs must look at other sources of data and dig deeper into what Kathryn Parker Boudett, Elizabeth City, and Richard Murnane refer to as the *problem of practice* (Boudett, City, & Murnane, 2005).

The *problem of practice,* according to Boudett et al. (2005), follows from first identifying what they refer to as a *learner-centered problem.* Teacher teams focus first on finding out where students have missed the mark and then drill down into additional, more specific data to pinpoint where the breakdown in instruction occurred. This breakdown is the *problem of practice.* It is directly linked to a specific *learner-centered problem* and can only be clearly identified by funneling down from the macrodata (e.g., EOC results) to the microdata (e.g., gaps in what students practiced and assessment content).

It is often the case that the value of any particular type of data as a source of information for identifying the problem of practice and improving instruction is proportional to the frequency with which the data type is collected. Summative data garnered once yearly from state assessments are limited in what they can reveal about the problem of practice compared to CFA data or daily classwork data. That is, the shorter the time intervals between "data harvests," the more opportunities teachers have to adjust their instruction and therefore the more useful it is. In schools that examine only annual state data, very little is likely to happen at the classroom level to impact instruction based on that data. For example, it is not useful for teachers to learn that students performed poorly on a language arts standard involving figurative language without examining how those teachers taught figurative language as well as how they assessed student mastery of figurative language.

For this reason, schools must abandon end-of-year data as the principle data source and must instead be in the habit of constantly reviewing available data as they become available throughout the school year. This is the work of the PLC. Consider the following data pyramid, modified from Stiggins, Arter, Chappuis, and Chappuis (2010).

Figure 5.2 illustrates the summative and formative data sources reviewed by the PLC and by individual teachers with regard to the frequency and relative usefulness of the data. Data sources high on the pyramid occur infrequently and tend to have limited usefulness in impacting instruction, while those sources lower in the pyramid occur more frequently and are more useful.

Figure 5.2 Data Pyramid (Frequency and Usefulness)

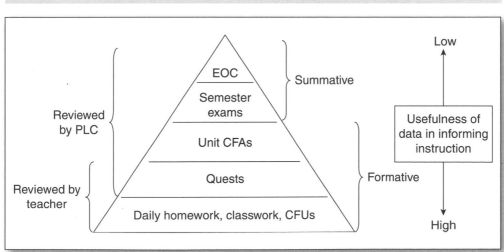

Looking at the Data

In reviewing available data, PLCs proceed from the macrodata to the microdata. Starting with the least frequent and most general source of data—typically state assessment results—PLCs begin by looking for patterns and gaps in student performance.

As teachers recognize these patterns and gaps, they do so initially without inference; that is, it is essential for PLCs to make factual observations about what is present in the data and resist the temptation to accompany observations with probable causes. The rush to *why* often skews objectivity in looking at *what* is present. There is a natural tendency to view data through the lens of preexisting expectations and assumptions and jump to the myriad of possible reasons for gaps that are observed. When this happens, teachers tend to look at the data with bias, anticipating possible causes prematurely. This is problematic because identifying the causes leads to corrective action; if the cause is misidentified, the resulting action will likely be ineffective.

So, the question to first ask when looking at data early in the process is not *"What do we think is going on here?"* but rather *"What do the data show? What do we see in the data?"* Only after asking this query and having a discussion of what is present should PLCs dig more deeply in the data to look for evidence that might explain the gaps. To be sure, inferences will need to be made—just not right away.

To help PLCs separate descriptive and inferential analyses of data, I recommend the *Notice & Wonder Protocol* (see Figure 5.3).

Figure 5.3

Notice & Wonder Protocol

A protocol for analyzing data both descriptively and inferentially.

Time: 40 minutes

1. Participants are presented with a table and/or graph of data pertaining to their practice. The data set may be displayed on a screen for all to see, or it may be given to each PLC member in hardcopy form. (I prefer the former, since graphs and sometimes data in table form are often illustrated in color.)

2. Each participant is given a 5″ × 7″ index card. Quietly and individually, participants write three observations evident in the graph or table. These observations must be free of inference or speculation; they are factually based from objectively examining the display. Each observation starts with the phrase, *"I notice that. . . ."* (5 minutes)

3. *Round 1.* In turn, each participant reads aloud one new observation that has not yet been shared, each time beginning with the phrase, *"I notice that. . . ."* The facilitator records the responses on chart paper. After the last participant shares one new observation, the first participant offers a second new observation and the process continues until all observations have been shared aloud, *without discussion.* (5 minutes)

4. Each participant turns over his index card and quietly writes three speculations or question-statements based on the observations heard in Round 1. These speculations attempt to offer possible explanations for the observations or pose suggestions for pursuing additional data. No attempt should be made to *solve* the problems that surface; the intent is to gain insights into what the data suggest, how the data are connected, and what the data imply. Each speculation starts with the phrase, *"I wonder why. . . ."* or *"I wonder if. . . ."* (5 minutes)

5. *Round 2.* In turn, each participant reads aloud one new speculation that has not yet been shared, each time beginning with the phrase, *"I wonder. . . ."* The facilitator records the responses on chart paper. This process continues as in Round 1 until all speculations have been shared aloud, *without discussion.* (10 minutes)

6. *Discussion.* PLC members discuss what has been shared and possible causes, connections, and links to classroom instruction and note other additional data that may be needed. (15 minutes)

To illustrate how this protocol might look in the presence of data, consider Figures 5.4a and 5.4b, which depict trends in a particular school's Grade 4 reading scores as they compare with district and state results.

Figure 5.4a   Sample Data for *Notice & Wonder Protocol*: School, District, and State Comparison by Year

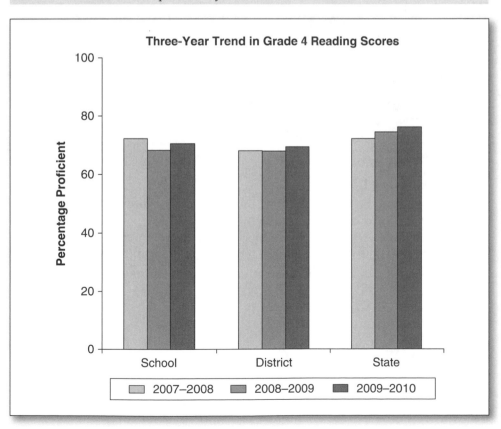

Figure 5.4b   Sample Data for *Notice & Wonder Protocol*: School, District, and State Comparison by Goal

2009–2010 Grade 4 Reading End-of-Grade Goal Summary Report				
	Goal Description Summary (The learner will. . . .)	Percentage of Test Items	School Percentage Proficient	Difference From District Mean Percentage	Difference From State Mean Percentage
Goal 1	Apply enabling strategies and skills to read and write.	13%	77	6	−1
Goal 2	Apply strategies and skills to comprehend text that is read, heard, and viewed.	26%	63	−2	−11
Goal 3	Make connections through the use of oral language, written language, and media and technology.	20%	72	−1	−6
Goal 4	Apply strategies and skills to create oral, written, and visual texts.	23%	69	2	−5
Goal 5	Apply grammar and language conventions to communicate effectively.	18%	74	2	−4

During Round 1 of the protocol, PLC members offer observations about the data. In the case of our sample data (Figures 5.4a and 5.4b), teachers may make observations based on information from either the graph or the table, or they may choose to share observations that stem from synthesizing the two. An observation referencing only the graph (Figure 5.4a) might be, "I notice that the state Grade 4 reading scores have increased over the past three years while our district scores have remained relatively flat during this time." Alternatively, the observation, "I notice that our students did least well on Goal 2, which comprises the greatest percentage of test items," reflects information gleaned from the table in Figure 5.4b. Still other teachers may combine the information from both graphic sources and share something like this. "I notice that our kids performed the same as the district overall in 2009–2010, but they considerably outperformed the district in Goal 1." By going through the process in Round 1, teachers are compelled to really look at what the data are saying, without bearing the intellectual burden of having to explain why.

As teachers move into Round 2, they veer from making observations to making speculations or posing queries about what they see in the data. Examples of these might be as follows:

> I wonder if the three-year trends in reading scores are similar for Grades 3 and 5.
>
> I wonder if we're doing all we can be doing regarding the use of technology, particularly in light of our students' performance on Goal 3.
>
> I wonder if we're giving students enough practice opportunities with oral texts.
>
> I wonder if our high teacher turnover rate accounts for our school's inconsistent performance over the three years.
>
> I wonder why our kids are having difficulty with comprehension.
>
> I wonder what we might do differently, day to day, to help with comprehension.

By pushing teachers to think about causes for what they see in the data—only after they've extracted factual observations from it—the conversation evolves from what *has* happened to what they *might do* to address the issues that surface. That's not to say that areas of concern will be solved at this point, but that an important conversation has begun that acknowledges gaps. As Dr. Phil aphorizes, "You can't fix what you don't acknowledge." Such is the case with reviewing and responding to student data.

Coaches facilitating the *Notice & Wonder Protocol* will need to be strict in not allowing speculations to be offered during the first round. In a similar way, it is best to refrain from attempting to "fix" issues that may surface. The goal is to hone in on what the data are saying and identify what other information teachers might need to piece together a "data picture" of what is happening. During this process, PLCs will have to force themselves to be descriptive and questioning rather than too prescriptive.

The benefit of doing the *Notice & Wonder Protocol* is in having teachers take a detailed look at the many kinds of information that a table or graph can reveal. For many teachers, it may be the first time they have explored data this thoroughly. In Round 2, when the teachers ponder the "whys" and "ifs" of their observations, they are set up for the next phase of asking *exploratory questions* and eventually diving more deeply into the data and linking it to classroom practice.

Asking Exploratory Questions

Some of the items the team identifies on the Wonder list compiled in Round 2 can be answered definitively with a little checking. The PLC can dole out these items to individual members to check on and report back at the next meeting. For example, items like, "I wonder how many days coverage are allotted in the pacing guide for topic X," or "I wonder if the Honors section uses resource Y," can be checked easily and followed up on later. The remaining items on the Wonder list will take center stage as the team then groups these items by content. Most of the remaining Wonder items will fall into one of four broad categories: *Classroom Instruction, Classroom Assessment, Student-Produced Work* (both in and out of the classroom), and *Materials.*

Once the items are grouped, the PLC either as a whole group or in smaller groups (pairs or triads) collapses the areas into three or four exploratory questions that they deem most important to pursue. These questions are not necessarily all-encompassing; it is perfectly okay if some items on the Wonder list are not addressed by the questions. That the PLC chooses critical exploratory questions in addressing a learner-centered gap is more important than that the questions be all-encompassing. It may be the case, for example, that the list of Wonder items is disproportionately skewed to the Classroom Assessment category. In this case, the PLC would no doubt address how teachers are assessing the area of concern in one or more of the exploratory questions.

To illustrate the process of asking exploratory questions, as well as the processes explained in the sections that follow, consider the five-part case study of Jackson Middle School, a fictitious but representative urban school.

Jackson Middle School (Part 1)

Jackson Middle School (JMS) is an urban middle school of 1,280 students located in the greater Atlanta area. Five teachers, one of whom coaches the group, comprise the English 8 PLC. In reviewing last year's English 8 state EOC results, which are broken down by the five goals established for English 8 by the state of Georgia, team members realized that their students performed poorly on Goal 3, as compared to both state and district averages. At JMS, the percentage of students performing at a proficient level for Goal 3 was 46.7%, compared to district and state averages of 58.1% and 65.3%, respectively. JMS percentages for the other four goals also trailed state and local averages, but each did so by single digits. For JMS, Goal 3 was almost 12 percentage points behind the district and almost 20 points lower than the state average.

To gain insight as to what might be happening with Goal 3, they looked to the district-administered quarterly assessment results, which mimicked the state EOC in content and format, but provided proficiency percentages by subgoal. Using these two data reports, the state EOC percentages and the district assessment percentages, the English 8 PLC turned to the *Notice & Wonder Protocol* to generate exploratory questions.

The PLC made quick notice of the fact that Jackson students performed comparably to the district on three of the four subgoals under Goal 3. The fourth subgoal, *Drawing Inferences From Text*, was a clear exception, and team members wondered to what extent their students' performance on this subgoal was affecting their overall performance on Goal 3.

After completing the *Notice & Wonder Protocol* and categorizing Wonder items into the four groups, the PLC arrived at the following exploratory questions regarding Goal 3:

1. Why are our students not able to draw inferences from text?

2. What are we presently doing to teach them to draw inferences from text?

3. Where are the gaps in what we're requiring them to do regarding inference to what the Georgia EOC requires them to be able to do?

In a nutshell, members of the Jackson Middle School English 8 PLC needed to know why what they were doing to teach inference was ineffective and what they could be doing additionally. To answer these questions, the English 8 PLC needed to dig into additional data.

PURSUING ADDITIONAL DATA

The English 8 PLC at Jackson Middle School identified a specific gap in the students' learning: drawing inferences from text. PLC members were confident that student performance on this subgoal significantly lowered their students' overall scores for Goal 3 in the state EOC assessment.

But identifying the student-learning gap is only a first step in the direction of solving and fixing the problem. They still needed to know *why* their students did poorly in this area and, in turn, what they were doing or not doing to cause the gap. That is, they needed to identify the problem of practice. To accomplish this, the English 8 PLC needed to pursue additional information.

Drilling Down Into the Data

The point of pursuing additional data is for the PLC to gather microdata in order to better understand current instructional gaps and thus fine tune the PLC's diagnosis of the problem. As the PLC moves from the macrodata to the microdata, team members begin to uncover smaller pieces of the puzzle that help them pinpoint where the breakdown is occurring in their students' learning.

The macrodata point them in the right direction; the microdata produce specific information that leads them to the modifications in instruction and assessment of that instruction that will amp up their students' learning.

To accomplish this, everything relevant to the identified learning gap must be brought to the foreground, out on the table for all to review.

This process is exemplified in Part 2 of the five-part case study of Jackson Middle School.

Jackson Middle School (Part 2)

In an attempt to answer their exploratory questions, members of the English 8 PLC gathered all artifacts relevant to how they taught and tested their students with respect to drawing inferences from text. The artifacts included previous lesson plans, copies of text used during instruction, in-class work assignments, homework assignments, quizzes, tests, activities, and samples of scored student work (from last year's students). Additionally, the team brought to the table the state-published indicators for Goal 3 as well as state-released EOC test items.

For the next two PLC meetings, the teachers used these artifacts to construct a cohesive picture linking the what, when, and how of their instruction. They learned what they had done to instruct their students to draw inferences, when and for how long their students worked on this learning objective, how they provided practice for their students, how they tested mastery, and how their assessments of mastery squared with state EOC test items for Goal 3.

By the end of the third PLC meeting completely focused on this specific problem area, the JMS English 8 PLC concluded the following:

1. The teachers spent too few days developing inference as a skill.

2. The pieces of text used for drawing inferences were exclusively of medium-level difficulty.

3. No opportunities were provided for students to draw inferences from text orally, without a written component.

4. Their CFAs and in-class assignments were limited to *Multiple-Choice* (choosing appropriate inferences), *Matching* (matching inferences to textual statements), and short *Fill-in-the-Blank* items using partially stated inferences provided by the teachers.

5. The student work samples failed to demonstrate the students' thinking as to why they selected the inferences they did in the *Multiple-Choice* and *Matching* tasks. The student work samples also revealed that students seemed unable to judge the reasonableness of the inferences they drew, that they seemed unaware of what makes an inference valid.

6. The content selected as text for drawing inferences was generally uninteresting to eighth-grade students.

Triangulating the Data

Any one piece of data is insufficient in describing what is happening regarding the identified learning gap. As the teachers of the JMS PLC investigated their students' lack of proficiency in drawing inferences, they physically brought to the table artifacts involving lessons, in-class work, homework, teacher-made assessments, and student work samples. This allowed them to fully understand the disconnect they observed between their instruction and their students' performance on the EOC assessment of Goal 3. This is critical. Without carefully examining all of these relevant artifacts, the PLC risks failing to see the inconsistencies present in these items. All essential data must be linked to other relevant data for a complete picture to emerge. Only then can PLCs connect gaps in their students' learning to gaps in teacher instruction.

Connecting Learning Gaps to Instructional Gaps

All too often, teachers use data to discover where their students are weak or to identify skills and concepts their students have not mastered, and then they stop there. In these instances, teachers are seeing only half of the issue. Unless and until teachers link these student weaknesses to teacher practice, that is, to *instructional* weaknesses, they cannot move forward in fixing the problem. The teachers who comprise the JMS English 8 PLC did just that.

Jackson Middle School (Part 3)

Team members learned how the in-class work they assigned students, as well as the assessments that were consistent with this work, failed to provide their students with opportunities to *construct their own inferences.* This left the teachers with no real sense of how their students reasoned from text to conclusions about implications present in the text. *Multiple-Choice* and *Matching* items, like those given by the English 8 PLC, were limited in that the inferences from the text were provided—albeit along with some flawed ones—and that all appropriate inferences were already constructed by the teachers. *Choosing* an appropriate inference, the team realized, was a significantly different skill than *drawing* an appropriate inference. And while the *Multiple-Choice* items may have mimicked the format of the state EOC assessment in a summative way, these items provided teachers with little formative information about how their students were learning to draw inferences.

When the teachers took a hard look at the kinds of texts used during their instruction of inference, they saw that all of the text was of the same medium-level difficulty. This alerted them to the fact that their instruction of the skill of drawing inferences was not developed in any real sense; instruction failed to proceed from easy to more difficult passages as students acquired the skill. In this way, team members simultaneously expected too much and too little of their students with regard to this skill.

Additionally, PLC teachers decided that more student-interesting texts could be selected in lieu of the passages they had used about U.S. fuel consumption or the mating habits of panda bears in captivity. Topics like these were used without question, no doubt because the content was interesting to the adults.

TRANSLATING DATA INTO ACTION

Planning a Course of Action

It would be hard to overemphasize the gravity of conducting the previously discussed phases of inquiry *before* rushing to a plan of action. Without laying out the relevant artifacts and identifying specific instructional shortfalls, JMS English 8 PLC teachers could not have developed a targeted course of action to improve their students' skills in drawing inferences. This is a paramount change in the way teachers customarily look at data. A cursory review of the macrodata, immediately followed by a rush to action, will never produce a viable solution to the learning problem. The plan to act must be sculpted from having chipped away at the big chunks of useful information and from having chiseled the details until the solution takes clear form. Once this is done, without rushing the process, the specific instructional gaps will become so evident that the plan of action will all but write itself. In the case of Jackson Middle School, after the English 8 PLC teachers did the necessary prework outlined in Parts 1–3, they were ready to make a viable plan to correct the learner-centered problem.

Jackson Middle School (Part 4)

In the fourth PLC meeting strictly dedicated to improving their students' mastery of what they deemed the most urgent area of concern, drawing inferences from text, the JMS English PLC teachers were ready to write a plan of action to correct the learning gaps. They decided on the following:

1. Two additional days would be spent on teaching inference, raising the number of days covered from three to five.

2. The instructional unit would begin by students reading a single paragraph of text and drawing inferences orally from the text. Each of the five days of instruction would begin with students reading a paragraph and drawing oral inferences. This would be done as a whole class, then in pairs, then by individual students.

3. The teachers would rewrite their assessments on drawing inferences so that 50%–60% percent of the questions would be constructed-response items in which students would be required to write their own inferences from textual

passages. At least half of the remaining 40%–50% percent of the items would require students to explain their reasoning for choosing the inferences on *Multiple-Choice* and *Matching* questions

4. In-class assignments would be structured in accord with the new assessments, except that in all cases of *Multiple-Choice* and *Matching* questions, student would be required to defend their choices by citing specific passages from the text.

5. During instruction, students would be taught characteristics of good inferences and these characteristics would be converted to an Inference Rubric with which students would evaluate their own and their classmates' inferences. Teachers would use this same Inference Rubric for scoring test items.

6. Teachers would spend a PLC meeting brainstorming new, more interesting content for text choices. Articles about social networking, sports, and music were among the possible topics to consider. As text is gathered, team members decided they would categorize passages by difficulty: easy, medium, and challenging.

7. Opportunities for students to draw inferences would not end with the unit test. Teachers agreed that at least once every other week, the class *warm-up* would consist of a textual passage with which students would anonymously write and defend an inference on index cards. Teachers would collect and redistribute the cards for students to evaluate one another's inference and evidence using the Inference Rubric.

In addition to deciding what needed to be done to close the observed learning gaps in their students, the English 8 PLC teachers attached a time frame and names of members of the PLC to the seven items listed in Part 4 of the Jackson Middle School case study. Doing this assures that the items proposed actually get done and that they are done in a time-bound manner. The PLC coach leads the conversation about who does what and when it is reasonable to expect completion of the individual and collective tasks.

Planning an Evaluation Measure

Just as it is important to put into writing a time-bound plan of action, so too is it necessary to decide at the outset how its effectiveness will be measured. Specifically, PLC teachers will need to decide what artifacts will constitute evidence that their plan is working (has worked) to make a positive impact on their students' learning of the area identified. Scored student work is central to these artifacts. By contrasting the new student work samples with the old work reviewed during the data inquiry phase, teachers can see concrete gains in student learning.

The JMS English 8 PLC teachers decided that, after the first three days of instruction on inferences, they would come together and review samples of all student work produced relating to drawing inferences. This included student inferences drawn during class warm-ups, student work on five written assignments (three easy-level and two medium-level passages), and scored quizzes given on the first half of the unit. Team members planned to meet again at the close of the instructional unit to assess their students' progress. During this second meeting, they would bring additional student work, including the CFA results, for review.

Implementing the Plan of Action

Of course, the work doesn't end in the planning of a course of action. At some point, what teachers write in their plan will need to be done. As alluded to in the JMS illustration, the PLC coach will lead a discussion about who will do what and when. Some items on the plan of action will be done by the PLC as a whole, others will be done by all members, but individually, and other tasks will be completed only by individual teachers to later share with the whole PLC. For the JMS English 8 PLC, ownership of the plan of action broke down as follows.

Jackson Middle School (Part 5)

Done as a whole PLC

- Revising the pacing guide to reflect the two additional days of instruction on inference
- Rewriting the CFA and deciding what to keep from the old assessments
- Rewriting the in-class assignments
- Brainstorming topics for textual passages
- Categorizing textual passages by difficulty
- Writing the characteristics of a good inference and sculpting a rubric

Done by all members, individually

- Finding interesting texts of varied difficulty
- Executing the instructional changes, such as the warm-ups
- Teaching the characteristics of a good inference and using the rubric with students
- Keeping a record of student performances on in-class work and on the CFA

Done by certain individual members

- Selecting text for the warm-ups
- Writing quiz and test items to share with the group

Looping Back (to Reviewing Existing Data)

Once the PLC evaluates the effectiveness of the implemented plan of action with regard to improving student learning of the targeted learning outcome, it is ready to repeat the process with a new target area. PLC teachers do this much the way they did it the first time: by looping back to the macrodata and reviewing that existing data for observable gaps in student learning. In this way, the PLC is continually working on improving some aspect of student learning. Sometimes, as in the case with Jackson Middle School, the target area will be a curricular component that demonstrates gaps in student learning. Other times, the target will be a subgroup of students who are not performing proficiently in a certain area. For example, it may be that students generally do well in solving first-degree linear equations in an algebra class, but when the data are disaggregated, it becomes clear that economically disadvantaged kids are performing significantly worse than their more affluent counterparts. By looping back to the start of the process and leaving no stone unturned, PLCs can identify and address these gaps in their students' learning.

SUMMARY: DATA

Using data to make important instructional changes is a layered process that starts with reviewing the big data, the macrodata. By asking exploratory questions and pursuing other relevant microdata, PLCs refine their inquiry until they pinpoint specific learning gaps in their students' mastery of the area of concern. These gaps lead PLC teachers to identify gaps in their instruction or the problem of practice (Boudett & Steele, 2007).

Before rushing to corrective measures, the PLC lays out a detailed plan of action that is both time-bound and accompanied by a plan to measure effectiveness. Once ownership of the plan's components is parceled out to individual members—or to the whole PLC—the plan is put into action, after which new data are gathered (in the form of teacher and student artifacts) to judge its effectiveness.

If the evidence suggests that the plan has worked and that student learning has increased—that the team has "fixed" the problem of practice and eliminated learning gaps—the PLC loops back to reviewing existing data and commences to tackle a new area in which student learning can be improved.

When PLC teachers begin to use data in this way, they begin to view all collaborative endeavors through the lens of improving and focusing on student learning and evidence of that learning. Looking at teacher and student work (Essential Task No. 1) and designing quality CFAs (Essential Task No. 2) become part of the data mosaic that informs the PLC about what needs to be done and how teachers should proceed in doing it to improve the quality and quantity of learning for all students.

PART III

COACHING AUTHENTIC PLCs

When CES spearheaded CFGs in the early 1990s, senior staffers such as Paula Evans, Gene Thompson-Grove, and Mary Hibert-Neuman spent an enormous amount of energy training those teacher leaders who would facilitate the CFGs in their respective schools. Collaboration is, after all, a human endeavor, and plotting a course through the complexities of such work requires a facilitator who is skilled in the ways of interpersonal navigation. Somewhere during the metamorphosis from CFG to PLC, facilitation skills have taken a back seat to the relentless drive for student results. I have learned that, without adequately training PLC coaches, this drive for results is all too often more bumpy and less effective than it has to be.

This final part is for the coaches. We consider in Chapter 6 suggestions for executing to full benefit the protocols and activities mentioned in previous chapters, as well as adding two new ones for coaches to "pull out" as they feel necessary in leading their PLCs. Chapter 6 concludes with a Frequently Asked Questions (FAQ) section, addressing questions of relatively minor significance that I'm often asked in working with PLC coaches. In Chapter 7, we proceed in discussing a few selected issues that necessitate more detailed discussions. But first, I feel compelled to offer a word for thought from my lessons in the trenches coaching PLCs. The sentiment that follows, in my view, gets at the heart of being an effective PLC coach.

It's Not About You

If there is anything I have learned from the host of amazing facilitators with whom I have had the pleasure to work at CES, it is this: It's not about me. It's not about what I know; it's not about who I know; it's not about the clarity I have for the work we do. It's about where the participants of my PLC are. It's about guiding them from where they are, complete with their ambitions, their naiveté, and their fears, to the next higher step in being an effective, collaborative team. It's about balancing the needs of individual members with the need to honestly look at our teaching and do right by our students. When PLC coaches see themselves as catalysts for good and important change, they see themselves less as managers of people and more as conduits for making their PLCs an effective, collective entity that happens to be made up of individual teachers.

Each teacher in a PLC brings to the table her own expertise, her own style, and her own readiness to do her part in this collaborative entity whose uncompromising focus shall always be on student learning. Everything else that a PLC coach does is but a means to achieve this important end. As coaches, we must constantly remind ourselves that it's not about where I am in my thinking and readiness to move forward; it is about where my PLC teachers are in their individual and collective thinking and readiness to move forward.

6

Coach's Guide to Facilitating Protocols and Activities

In this chapter, I highlight a few key points for effectively facilitating some of the protocols discussed throughout this book, provide two additional protocols that are particularly well suited in assisting coaches in honing the interpersonal aspects of their PLCs, and address some commonly asked questions of PLC coaches doing the work.

PROTOCOLS FOR TEAM BUILDING, NORM SETTING, AND CONSTRUCTING COMMUNITY KNOWLEDGE

Traffic Jam

(See steps in Chapter 2.) The discussion that follows this activity is central to its success and to its relevance to PLCs. After the task is accomplished, the coach asks the PLC this: *What does this activity have to do with being a part of an authentic PLC?* The participants share their responses and the coach records them on chart paper. As participants share parallels to

PLCs, coaches capitalize on selected responses by asking follow-up questions like these: *Can you say more? What makes you think that?*

Some common parallels include the following:

- Communicating
- Working together (teamwork)
- Not giving up until successful
- Seeing the emergence of leaders and followers
- Making multiple attempts before being successful
- Following the rules/procedure (like group norms, protocols)
- Solving problems
- Trusting each other

Some less common and more thoughtful parallels include the following:

- Focusing on the good of the group and not on the good of the individuals
- Dealing with elements of frustration
- Working with the varied comfort levels of team members
- Trusting the process and trusting that success *is* possible
- Being confused at times
- Disagreeing with each other at times
- Responding to data and adjusting behavior
- Showing great elation in eventually succeeding

As coach, be sure to get at these more thoughtful parallels, even if you have to volunteer a few items yourself.

Norm-Setting Protocol

(See steps in Chapter 2.) One of the tricky parts of facilitating this protocol is in grouping the suggestions for norms into like categories. Coaches will have to think on their feet and take care to sort norms by their meanings and not by key words that are used. For example, a norm suggestion to *"Respect start and stop times"* may not fit with one suggesting to *"Respect differing opinions,"* despite the common use of "respect." The first norm may best fit in a general *Norms for PLC Meetings* category while the second might be well-placed in the *Norms for Having Discussions* group of suggestions.

Coaches will need to encourage comfort with Part 4 of the protocol, which calls for dissenting opinions about the norm suggestions. Most teachers are reluctant to disagree with a norm suggestion of a colleague, even if they are quietly thinking the norm isn't feasible or even desirable. I observed a PLC using this protocol and heard one teacher suggest on her index card to "keep all conversations upbeat and positive." While that may sound like a great idea on the surface, one wise teacher in the group challenged the norm, suggesting that there well may be times during which the conversations of the PLC aren't so upbeat and positive as teachers engage in the hard work of discussing instructional issues or closely examining student work. Once he challenged the suggestion and explained his reasoning, the rest of the group readily agreed. As we enter Part 4 of the *Norm-Setting Protocol,* I tell my PLCs to challenge any norm they can't live with or don't agree with. I tell them that we all have to "live with the list we come up with" and that challenging a norm "gives us good practice with separating the work (the suggestion) from the person (the teacher who suggested the norm)." After making such comments at the front end, it is hard for a teacher to be put off by having her norm challenged.

Text-Based Discussion Protocol

(See steps in Chapter 2.) Once the discussion begins, the biggest challenge in facilitating is keeping the focus on the text and not on the host of other things teachers tend to want to talk about. A text-based discussion can quickly turn into an open discussion, dominated by one or two vocal teachers, whose comments may diverge from the text. To steer clear of this, the coach can do the following:

- Refocus the group by referring back to the text.
- Ask another teacher, beforehand, to go back to the text and make a comment if she sees the discussion veering away from the text.
- Have copies of the Text-Based Discussion Guidelines available for teachers.
- Read the Text-Based Discussion Guidelines before beginning, having individual volunteers read one guideline each.
- Remind participants to model going back to the text rather than admonishing a teacher for straying from the text.
- Remind participants to refrain from autobiographical comments.
- Remind participants to keep comments relatively short.
- Ask the following of teachers whose comments stray from the text: *Can you tell us where you are in the text? How does the author address this?*
- Choose text that is interesting and relatively short (no longer than a short article).

PROTOCOLS FOR TEACHER AND STUDENT WORK AND ISSUES AND DILEMMAS

Tuning Protocol, Consultancy, and Charette Protocols

(See steps of each in Chapter 3.) These three protocols all involve either looking at teacher or student work or helping a teacher with an issue,

dilemma, or obstacle he is facing in his work. It is helpful for coaches to keep the following in mind as they provide their PLCs effective leadership in these areas.

- Have copies of the steps of the protocols available for all PLC members.
- Adhere to the steps of the protocols and read each aloud as you transition from one step to the next.
- Adhere to the times indicated for each step, with the possible exception of Step 4 in the *Tuning Protocol*, which may be shortened depending on the type of work being examined.
- At the beginning of each protocol, remind the PLC of the goal of the protocol.
- When finishing one segment and moving to the next, allow ample time for participants to make one more comment.
- Model being comfortable with pauses of silence.
- Remind participants to allow space for those asking probing questions as there may be a follow-up question.
- Remind participants to focus on the work being presented and not on the presenter as a person.
- Listen and take notes while people are speaking.
- Equalize "air time" among participants.
- Publicly acknowledge good clarifying and probing questions as exemplars for participants.
- Remind participants to refrain from autobiographical comments.
- Remind participants at the onset to respect the vulnerability of the presenter(s).
- Remind the presenter at the end that she is expected to offer an update of work at the start of the next meeting.
- During the debriefing process, thank the presenter and ask for her reflections first.
- During the debriefing process, focus the team on the process and remind them that the segments for comments related to content are over.
- Be careful to pick the appropriate protocol for the work in question.

TWO FACILITATOR PROTOCOLS

As coaches, we must be continually attuned with the interpersonal dynamics of our PLCs. We know that effective collaboration depends on our keen awareness of how the PLC is functioning as a team. PLC members don't have to think about such things; this responsibility falls squarely on the shoulders of coaches. Everything that the PLC does in impacting student achievement happens in the context of human interaction and the coach must recurrently assess how things are going in this regard so that the work of the PLC is done well.

Two protocols that can assist coaches in this endeavor—to take pulse of and hone the interpersonal skills of their PLCs—are the *Inquiring Introductions* and *Hopes & Fears Protocols.* Coaches can use these at any time to encourage PLCs to check in with each other and unite in their mission to impact learning.

Inquiring Introductions Protocol

Anne E. Jones, a postdoctoral student at Harvard Graduate School of Education and a colleague of mine, developed this protocol (see Figure 6.1). It invites PLC members to listen actively to each other as they respond in question form to what was last stated by a colleague. All members of a

Figure 6.1

Inquiring Introductions Protocol

An activity to sharpen the listening and questioning skills of members in a PLC. Developed by Anne E. Jones.

Time: 35–45 minutes (depending on group size)

Procedure:

1. Participants form groups of four to six people.

2. Each participant quietly writes on an index card his responses to the following:
    a. Full name
    b. Subject and/or grade level taught (or title, if the participant is in a support position)
    c. One vacation experience you have had or plan to have (one or two sentences)

3. Rounds.
    Each round begins with one member of the group being designated the *Introducer,* who shares the information on her card. After the Introducer makes her introduction by sharing her card, another participant asks a question of the Introducer, who answers the question in a sentence or two (no more than a brief paragraph).
    When she finishes answering the question, a second participant will ask the Introducer a follow-up question. The Introducer answers this question with a brief response. After she does this, a third participant asks a new follow-up question based on the response heard. The Introducer will respond and the next participant asks a follow-up question and so on until all members have asked a single question of the Introducer, who responds to each.
    The Catch: Each question that is asked must be *directly related* to the most recent statement made by the Introducer, namely, the last statement she made in response to the previous participant's question.
    Each member of the group takes a turn being the Introducer, with each of the other participants asking a question in turn.

PLC can benefit from trying it, but it is particularly well suited for PLC coaches as they develop the skill of intentional listening to contributions made by members of their PLC. Having experienced this protocol under the careful facilitation of Anne E. Jones, I can attest to the fact that it is most interesting and fun to do as it achieves its purpose. A PLC coach must be a really intent listener; this protocol is both simple and deliberate in its ability to compel first-class listening and questioning skills from participants.

What seems like a complicated procedure is actually quite simple and flows naturally as questions are alternately asked and answered. What is less natural for participants is having to abide by the restriction that only questions relating to the last thing said may be asked. This forces participants to really listen to what is being said and to avoid forming a question before the Introducer has completed answering the previous question. I recommend this protocol to all CPLCs, as it will help them in their leadership roles as coaches.

Hopes & Fears Protocol

This protocol, modified from a version in Joe McDonald and colleagues' *The Power of Protocols* (2007), brings to light fears that PLC members might be experiencing about their work. Again, part of being in an authentic PLC is having the courage to face those things that might be impeding progress. Whether these things relate to the work itself or to the institutional constraints that affect the work, it is sometimes advisable to stop and take note of those things that get in the way of putting student learning first and therefore impact the fundamental goal of improving student learning.

This protocol requires skillful facilitation on the part of the coach. Teacher discussions about what is problematic can quickly turn into counterproductive grumble sessions that solicit a sense of helplessness from participants. The point here is not to simply vent frustrations but to put on the table genuine obstacles that may be impeding their progress. Coaches should be on guard for a disproportionate number of obstacles mentioned that are out of the realm of control by the PLC. The reverse proportion is desirable; many more items should be mentioned over which the PLC has some control rather than no control.

It is noteworthy that the time allotted for the Hopes segment is a fraction of the time allotted for the Fears segment. This is by design. Hopes tend to be positive and serve to affirm the PLC's purpose and reason for being. Fears acknowledge that this is hard work and that there will be challenges along the way. The exchange between participants during the Fears segment is where the primary value of the protocol resides. In many instances, the items listed as hopes are also fears. This is normal. The point is not to solve every issue but to lay the issues on the table and gain

Figure 6.2

Hopes & Fears Protocol

Modified from the version suggested in The Power of
Protocols *by McDonald, Mohr, Dichter, and McDonald (2007)*

Time: 60 minutes

Purpose: To bring to light hopes and fears associated with trying something new that requires change or modification to existing ways of doing things. To offer suggestions to overcome obstacles—actual or anticipated—that may impede progress.

Procedure:

1. The facilitator gives each participant two index cards. (5 minutes)

On the first index card, participants silently write two hopes they have for the work being considered or work that is under way. A question-prompt for writing Hopes is this: *If this new idea/endeavor works as planned, what are the likely benefits of doing it?*

On the second index card, they write two fears they have associated with the work. A question-prompt for writing Fears is this: *If this new idea/endeavor doesn't go or isn't going as planned, what are the dangers or obstacles that may result or are present?*

2. The facilitator collects the cards, shuffles them, and redistributes the Hopes cards back to the group.

3. Without divulging the author, each participant reads aloud the Hopes on the index card he has been given. These are shared without discussion. (5 minutes)

4. Without divulging the authors, the facilitator reads aloud the Fears index cards and invites a brief discussion (3–4 minutes) after each. The goal of the discussion is to promote a deeper understanding of the fears, provide solutions where appropriate (though this is not necessary for each card), and suggest things that might be done to alleviate or avoid the circumstances that are fearful. (45 minutes)

5. The process is debriefed and any unattended fears are placed in the *Parking Lot** for future consideration as the group moves forward with the work. (5 minutes)

*The *Parking Lot* is a piece of chart paper generally posted in the PLC meeting room on which participants write issues or concerns that have not been fully addressed or resolved but can be temporarily "parked" so that the group can continue to move forward. (I have participants write concerns on sticky notes and place those on the *Parking Lot* chart paper so that the notes can be removed when the concerns are later resolved.)

insight from each other into what might be done to avoid, lessen, or work with the potential or actual obstacles. Figure 6.3 illustrates some examples of Hopes and Fears.

When individuals on the teams hear each others' Hopes and Fears, they get immediate confirmation that what they're hoping and fearing is

Figure 6.3   Sample Hopes and Fears

Examples of Hopes

    I hope that we become a tighter-knit faculty as a whole.

    I hope students become the primary benefactors of this.

    I hope fewer students will "fall through the cracks" by doing this work.

Examples of Fears

    I fear that student achievement might not improve.

    I fear that some of our teachers will resist this idea and not open up.

    I fear that the administration will try to direct too much and not let us do for ourselves.

---

not at all unique but shared by their colleagues. Even if every fear is not solved during the *Hopes & Fears Protocol,* it can be team uniting and somewhat therapeutic for members to be part of this process. It is comforting to know that other PLC members worry about whether student achievement will really improve or whether other coaches experience resistance from their PLC members. This is not to undervalue their concerns; the CPLC can address some of these issues more fully later, perhaps using a *Consultancy Protocol.* The time a PLC spends engaging in a the *Hopes & Fears Protocol* is well worth the effort. It also serves to give coaches a structured opportunity to learn where their PLCs are in terms of their attitudes and perspectives about doing the work.

The *Hopes & Fears Protocol* can be quite powerful. Though many issues shared by members are addressed in mostly cursory ways, the concerns are nonetheless put on the table. The effect of this is to honor individual voices in the team and also to unite the whole as the team responds to concerns by other members who had similar issues and dealt with them successfully. This sharing and solving aspect stands to be another way in which the team constructs community knowledge.

In working with PLC coaches, I am often asked common questions regarding some of the nuances in facilitating PLCs in general and protocols in particular. For brevity's sake, I address these concerns in the FAQ format that follows.

FREQUENTLY ASKED QUESTIONS

As the coach of my PLC, I find myself doing all the work. I write and type the agendas; I draft minutes after the meetings; I pick articles for us to discuss, etc. I can't even get everyone to do their readings before meetings, let alone do anything else for the group. How can I get them to do more or even their part?

The first half of your first sentence is telling. You refer to the PLC as "my PLC" instead of "our PLC," and that mentality is reflected in the distribution of labor. Stop doing all the work. Like students in the classroom, if teachers do all the work, then students become quite passive and expect us to do for them. The same phenomenon happens with teachers in PLCs.

Instead of choosing a reading assignment for teachers to read and discuss, use a sign-up sheet for teachers to pick the readings for the next three months, or copy the table of contents from the latest issue of *Educational Leadership* and have members individually choose the top three articles of greatest interest. Then decide together which ones will be read and who will be responsible for getting the articles to the group.

Teachers can rotate duties like taking minutes and typing up agendas. Coaches can ask a different member at the start of each meeting to read aloud the group norms. As coach, you'll get more buy-in and more commitment when PLC members take turns in the workload and have a voice in what is decided.

ℰℛ

We tried a Tuning Protocol using the work one teacher brought. The feedback was "flat" and there were awkward moments of silence. What am I doing wrong? What should I do?

It is common to feel as though your first *Tuning Protocol* was a bit flat. Not to worry. Remember, you're breaking new ground. Teachers are not used to the formality of the structure and they are usually very reluctant to offer cool feedback (despite the step in the protocol specifically calling for it). As coach, the best thing you can do is to trust the process. There is a temptation to alter the steps in the protocol following an initial "flat" experience. Don't do it. Be militant about the process. It will work. It is not uncommon for the second experience a team has with the *Tuning Protocol* to show marked strides in the quality of the exchanges.

As for moments of silence, provided teachers were engaged and not visibly uninterested, silence is often a sign of deep thinking. When I observe a PLC during a *Tuning Protocol,* I can gauge how seasoned the coach is by her comfort with stretches of silence. Silence is a good thing; don't feel compelled to have to say something and fill it in. The PLC's comfort with the pauses will increase with your comfort with silence.

However, if two or three consecutive *Tuning Protocol* experiences are as flat as the first, you will need to be more proactive in getting teachers to go deeper (see *Pushing the Conversation Deeper* in Chapter 7).

ℰℛ

Teachers are constantly arriving late to PLC meetings, sometimes by as much as 10 minutes. This is disruptive and causes me to have to repeat myself at the start of each meeting. What can I do to address this without pointing fingers?

You might try saying something at the end of the next meeting such as, "You all are aware that people are having trouble getting to the meetings on time. Should we push back the start time to ____?" If the consensus of the team is to change the start time, then do so. And then make certain you start the next meeting right on time, regardless of how many members are missing. If this is not the consensus, then announce following: "Ok, we'll stick to our present start time. I promise to do a better job starting the meeting right on time." And then make certain you start the next meeting right on time, regardless of how many members are missing.

If your PLC has a group norm of starting and ending meetings on time, it is advisable to remind team members that you all agreed to this. If there is no such norm, you might add it yourself the next time norms are being updated.

Teachers tend to stroll in and arrive late to meetings if they know you'll either wait for them or repeat for them what was said. Don't do either. As a last resort, pass out the sign-up sheet for duties at the very start of the meetings, leaving tardy members to get last pick. I predict they'll start coming on time.

ℬℚ

Shouldn't all members of the PLC be participating during a Tuning Protocol?

Yes, all members of the PLC should be participating to the extent that they are engaged in the process and with the work being presented. That doesn't imply that the PLC should necessarily hear from every member during each protocol. Teachers can be hesitant to speak, especially for first or second experiences with the protocol; silent doesn't mean disengaged. If there are members of the PLC who never speak, even after the team has experienced several protocols, then I would talk with those teachers individually to see if their silence is indicative of a problem. Silence can indicate recalcitrance, passive aggression, or reflection. Coaches have to make a judgment call in each case of teacher silence and address it accordingly.

ℬℚ

The same two or three teachers present work during the five protocols we have done in looking at student work. Should I, as coach, use a rotating list so that all members have a turn presenting?

For the *Tuning Protocol* to be authentic in terms of actually helping a teacher with her practice, it is important for teachers to present work when they feel they have something that truly needs help. That implies that a rotating list is probably not a good idea. Also, the first time teachers present (are in the "hot seat"), they must be ready for the risks and vulnerabilities that go with that. Only they can decide when they are ready.

That said, it is important for members to realize that each will have a turn in the "hot seat"; therefore, it is a good idea for them to volunteer as soon as they feel they are ready and as soon as they have a piece of work that could use some "tuning." There are teachers who may never volunteer to present, left to their own accord, but with a gentle nudge from a sensitive coach, usually find the courage to bring work. Speaking individually to such a teacher may be all it takes; for example, you could say the following: "We've had five *Tuning Protocols* so far; do you think you might feel comfortable bringing something for feedback next time?" Then it is advisable for the coach to meet with the teacher beforehand to go over what the teacher plans to bring, which protocol is best suited for the work, and what the teacher can expect. Easing the presenting teacher's mind is part of what coaches do to encourage the readiness of PLC members.

☙☙

My principal says that, at each meeting in which work is to be presented, members should all bring work and go around and share briefly what they brought. Then, the group as a whole should decide which work to "tune" in a Tuning Protocol. Is this a good way to decide?

No. While it is good practice to have all members bring work so that they demonstrate a tangible commitment to the PLC, it is not a good idea to have the group "vote" or otherwise decide who will present. Individual readiness to present will vary among members; having something good to present is not the same as being ready to be in the "hot seat." Only one person should decide when an individual teacher presents: the teacher herself. In addition to this reason, it turns out that in practice, teachers who are fearful to present avoid doing so by simply bringing the same sorry work each time—work that was not chosen during previous meetings.

☙☙

As coach of our PLC, is it ever appropriate to pass on the facilitation role to other members of the team? If so, when? And should I ask for volunteers?

Yes, it is appropriate to temporarily pass on the facilitator role to another member of the PLC. This is a decision the coach makes when he feels another member is ready and willing to facilitate and when the PLC as a whole stands to benefit from a temporary change in leadership. In addition to fostering growth of the new facilitator and the PLC as a whole, this also serves to form a beneficial alliance between the coach and the new facilitator when the role is returned to the coach. Having been in the facilitator role, the person develops an awareness of and becomes sympathetic to all the things the coach must do to effectively lead the PLC. This makes for a handy ally should the group dynamics later become challenging.

No, don't ask for volunteers. Coaches should decide who is ready to facilitate the team. I usually ask that person individually if he would like to facilitate a particular piece of the next meeting. Start small. There is no need to have a new person facilitate an entire *Tuning Protocol* at first chance; start by having a ready member facilitate one segment of a protocol, or lead the debriefing session of a *text-based discussion,* or lead the discussion during the updating of group norms, and so forth. The PLC coach should meet with the ready member and provide some guidance about leading the group. If it goes well, the new facilitator will build the confidence to try bigger bits in future meetings. If it does not go well, you're always there to jump in and save him. Be careful here though: Try your best to not chime in every time you think to yourself, "I would have facilitated that or answered this differently." Let the new person have at it and just make notes on those points you intend to bring up later when you debrief with him individually.

SUMMARY: COACHING PROTOCOLS

The PLC coach is the most essential component of a successful PLC. No matter how united the team or collaborative its work, members of the PLC will look to the coach for leadership in how the work is done, what gets prioritized, who takes responsibility for what, and so on. Although it is the entire PLC who owns the culture, it is the coach who maintains that culture. When coaches ask the hard questions and encourage team members to do the same, the PLC is pushed toward growth, and that growth translates into increased learning for students. Protocols can help enormously with the hard conversations, and PLCs quickly acquire comfort with the structure of those conversations.

Nowhere was I more convinced of this than at a middle school in rural South Carolina. I was contracted to consult 17 times throughout a single school year with the school's Leadership Team, a group of a dozen PLC coaches and the school's principal. We started at ground zero and built PLCs from the ground up. Due in large part to a committed and enthusiastic principal, within six months, the PLCs were deeply entrenched in the work of authentic PLCs and were already seeing measurable results in student achievement. The faculty became united in the common purpose of increasing learning for all kids by honestly discussing and improving instruction. They lived by the constant cycle of examining their work or the work of their students, responding to what they saw, and assessing the effectiveness of that response. Coaches led the way, using frequent protocols and continually monitoring the interpersonal dynamics of their groups until the culture of the teams transformed teacher isolation into interdependent collaboration. This all happened within the first six months.

Success for this school resulted in part from the PLC's willingness to try protocols and from the coach's preservation of the fidelity of the protocols by insisting that teams "trust the process." When PLCs keep their focus on improving work and not on merely going through the motions of engaging in protocols, members take note that these discussions *do* result in better work, and in turn, increased student learning. Coaches are key to this process.

In the final chapter, we look closely at larger issues that coaches face as they plot the course in moving their teams toward authenticity.

7

Troubleshooting Common Obstacles

As coaches and PLCs pursue the common goal of improving student learning by improving teacher practice, and as coaches in particular recognize and bear in constant mind that this pursuit is fundamentally interpersonal in nature, there are bound to be growing pains along the way. Some of these are relatively minor in the scheme of things and were addressed previously in the FAQ section in Chapter 6. Other obstacles, perhaps more burdensome but equally solvable, are discussed in greater detail in this final chapter.

COMMON OBSTACLES AND CHALLENGES

Dealing With Reluctant and Resistant Teachers

Before I launch into my best thoughts about how to deal with this most common and challenging aspect of coaching a PLC, it is necessary to mention that these two kinds of teachers are very different indeed; therefore, strategies to best deal with them are accordingly different.

Reluctant teachers are quite commonplace, especially in the early days of forming a working PLC. In fact, I have never known a PLC in which at least one member was not reluctant or skeptical to embrace the work and climate of a true PLC. Reluctant teachers are typically questioning and disagreeing—even downright negative at times—but they tend not to be ill-intentioned. That is, they aren't negative for reasons that stem from self-serving motives; they simply aren't "buying it" yet and need time to see the merits of the work before they are willing to invest their time and energy. They are *reluctant,* and they are less likely than other members to roll up their sleeves and give the new ideas a try. *Their motivation for their reluctance is doubt.*

Reluctant teachers respond best to a PLC coach who can "keep it real," who can appeal to their common sense, who shares successful cases of schools in which PLCs have made a difference, and who can illustrate the new ideas as these new ideas apply to real students in real schools with real teachers. Coaches who are able to convince them—in action and results and not in words—that PLCs work to make instruction more efficient and effective and that they lighten teacher loads, not add to them, are most successful in turning reluctant teachers into active, invested participants of the work.

Most reluctant teachers take longer to "come around" than other PLC members. They require more time in an effective collaborative environment before they are comfortable offering their contributions, especially cool feedback. If coaches act as patient facilitators and constantly remind themselves that it's about where the *teachers* are in terms of readiness, these reluctant teachers will usually come around. In the hands of a caring and effective coach, they nearly always do. Not surprisingly, formerly reluctant teachers often become the biggest advocates of the PLC and they often become ambassadors of PLC work for the rest of the faculty. When this happens, it is not uncommon for them to extol the virtues of PLCs, and in a few years they may well end up coaching a PLC of their own.

Some 20 years ago, I myself was a reluctant teacher. I questioned everything. I challenged everything. I had doubt. *Was this one more thing we've already tried, only to resurrect and repackage it with new catchphrases?* When I finally saw the difference and the impact of PLCs and the potential impact on my own students, I became the biggest advocate of the work (and remain so to this day). There is great elation in coaches who begin to see this transformation in the beliefs and attitudes of their reluctant PLC members. It's not unlike the elation of teachers who see eventual success in the achievements and attitudes of their struggling or negative students. Most every struggling student, once successful, will cite as his favorite teacher the one in whose class success triumphed over struggle.

In my experience, many reluctant teachers are actually very good in the classroom, and although their population is perhaps skewed to the more seasoned teachers, they are not always the veteran teachers. Sometimes it is the young and inexperienced teachers who question everything, due to a mix of naiveté, their fresh outlook on teaching, and even the generation to which they belong.

Resistant teachers are a wholly different trip from reluctant teachers. The good news is that they tend to be very few in number. The demographics of resistant teachers are very often characterized by teachers who have been in the system for many years, teachers who have become jaded through the years by having been disappointed one too many times by failing initiatives in which they *did* personally invest, or teachers who are resentful of advancements that have worked in which they chose not to be a part. They may be resentful a principal who is 20 years their junior. They may have extremely small and tightly defined comfort zones; anything happening outside those zones is viewed as a threat. They can at times be so negative about everything that one wonders if they even like kids at all, and one can't help but think that they remain in the profession only to see their way to retirement. Other times, they may be quite far from retirement, in midcareer, but they are seldom young or beginning teachers. Resistant teachers are in the habit of blaming everything outside of their small realm of control for the failures of their students. They seldom believe their own actions could be contributing to the failures of their students.

Truth be told, resistant teachers are often not very good in the classroom. And they usually know it. They sense that their colleagues know it, even though it is never discussed. They feel in their hearts that their principal believes it too, and that she has no genuine belief that they will ever be better. Resistant teachers are like unhappy spouses in bad marriages who hate their lot, but they will never leave and they won't do anything to change it. Instead, they become jaded and apathetic and would spend their energies sabotaging new ideas rather than trying to adopt them. *Their motivation for resistance is personal.*

Unlike the reluctant teachers who have doubts about the work itself, resistant teachers may have doubts about themselves. Their negative and often sarcastic exterior provides them a shield of protection for the poor teacher self-image that resides within. Think about it: If I am a resistant teacher, already feeling downtrodden and inadequate in my own teaching and in my effectiveness as a teacher, knowing that you know I'm not very good, and suddenly I'm asked to be part of a "real" PLC and put my work on the table for all to critically examine, how am I likely to react? Of course, I am going to do everything in my power to sabotage this threatening new idea at the earliest signs of where it might be going. This is not because I question its validity (like my reluctant counterparts) but because I feel compelled to protect myself and hold on dearly to my last thread of teacher dignity and self-worth. Does this same scenario not play out with resistant students in classrooms every day for exactly the same reasons? And what do the research and our own experiences tell us is the best way to handle such students?

Therein lies the solution. Resistant teachers will never respond to appeals exalting the merits of PLCs. They don't care about success statistics. They don't care about research. They may not even care about how PLCs stand to help student achievement. What they care about is themselves. This is not driven by ego so much as it is their drive of self-preservation.

The coach of resistant teachers must find ways to validate them as teachers. Resistant teachers tend to respond to *genuine* attempts to feed their teacher self-image by affirming them, appreciating their input, valuing their contributions, acknowledging the skills they do have, and so forth. Coaches must lean in and listen hard to the negative comments the resistant teachers offer. *What are they really saying?*

Most of all, coaches must go out of their way to *never ignore resistant teachers.* Never. Ignoring their negative comments is fuel to the resistant teacher's fire. Their words of sarcasm and resistance reflect their cries to be heard, to be acknowledged, and to be responded to, even if the response probes their thinking and motivations more deeply and challenges them to clarify their thinking. Try making comments such as these: *I'd like to know why you think that. Can you be more specific?* Or, *I think you make a good point about things beyond our control. But what, in your mind,* can *we do?* They'll get the message that negative comments *will* be validated but also explored. It is as if to say to them, "I care about you and your input too much to not ask you more about how and why you feel as you do, and because of that and my desire to keep things real, I'm going to call you on it." Resistant teachers change when the pain of staying the same becomes greater than the pain of changing (Fullan, 1993).

If strong but calm coaches respond to resistant teachers in this way, these teachers will either shut down (though this is not ideal, it is better than allowing them to contaminate the rest of the group), or they will, like the schoolhouse bully once stood up to, change their impetuous, negative attitude to one that is at least compliant. In time and with patience, they will usually join the ranks of the reluctant teachers who, with different approaches, eventually become participating and invested members of the group. Changes in beliefs are preceded by and are the result of changes in behavior (Evans, 2001). Therefore, coaches are well advised to strive to change resistant teachers' *behavior*—if only to one of compliance—than to attempt to first change their belief systems.

Many teachers who are categorized as resistant teachers by principals and PLC coaches are actually reluctant teachers. This is important to keep in mind, lest we miscategorize—and therefore mishandle—these different kinds of teachers who do not embrace the value of PLCs.

It is also true that there are those rare occasions in which some resistant teachers bring so much baggage and history to the scene that they may be too difficult for the coach to deal with effectively. If this is the case—and this is much less common than new coaches may think—then it becomes an administrative problem and it is up to the principal to step in and address those "hardcore" resistors. The PLC coach depends on the willingness of the members to try new ideas. As in the classroom with resistant students, there is a point at which teachers are spending too much energy on the resistors, often at the expense of the cooperative students, and this is a sign that administrative intervention is required.

That said, in most cases of reluctance and resistance, coaches can handle the matter effectively by understanding the differences between these two groups: Teachers in one group need to be convinced that this will work and teachers in the other group need to be convinced that they can be valuable and valued, in relative safety, in this work. As Robert Evans explains so perfectly in *The Human Side of School Change* (2001), most people change more often based on what that change means to them personally and less often because the change makes intellectual sense. Such is the way with resistant teachers.

Managing Conflict and Disagreement

In 1995, during my first year coaching a PLC (then called CFG) at the school where I was teaching, a heated debate occurred involving the purpose of assigning student homework. While I cannot recall the specifics of the disagreement, I do remember the two teachers in my CFG, ordinarily quiet to the point of disinterest, became vocal in their diametrically opposing viewpoints on the subject. I did my best to referee the situation, but I left the meeting feeling as though I was the most ineffective coach.

Frustrated by how things had gone at the meeting and not knowing what to do next to salvage my developing CFG, I called my personal CFG hero and mentor, Jude Pelchat. Jude was my facilitator when I was trained with the CES in 1993 and 1994. She was and remains to this day the very best facilitator with whom I have ever worked. I'll never forget her words of wisdom when I called to explain to her my dilemma. In her calm and wise way, she said something very close to this:

> Congratulations, Daniel. Your CFG just experienced its first significant growth spurt. Silence and passivity are the enemies of growth. Open disagreement is a key indicator of growth and trust. So long as neither party left the meeting with "hard feelings," you have nothing to worry about, or do, for that matter. In fact, if you pay particular attention to how these two teachers interact at the next meeting, you'll likely see a subtle, mutual respect.

Jude was right. Something transformative happened at the meeting in which the disagreement occurred. It was as if the mentality of the group became this: *We can disagree here. Be respectful. Don't get personal. But say what you're thinking. Get it on the table.*

Conflict and disagreement are going to happen at some point in every authentic PLC. But they are not the same thing. The difference, in a nutshell, is the presence of "hard feelings." Disagreements are healthy and necessary and generally void of hard feelings. Conflicts, on the other hand, are more unavoidable than they are necessary and are most often marked by hard feelings experienced by one or more persons.

DISAGREEMENTS + HARD FEELINGS = CONFLICT

Hard feelings result from taking things personally. Sometimes an issue is so dear to us as teachers that we become unable to hear differing perspectives without receiving them as personal attacks on our teacher character or on our teacher identities. When this happens—and it most often comes from a place of insecurity on our parts—we have great difficulty separating our sense of self from the differing opinion or perspective.

There is no easy solution for coaches facing these differences. But one thing coaches can do is insist that teachers involved in such conflicts refrain from interpreting differences as a personal affront and remind participants that they are to focus on the issues and not on the players involved in the issues. Coaches need to hark back to all members of the PLC that the barometer against which they measure the validity of all perspectives is what is best for student learning.

Of course, this is easier said than done. At times coaches will find themselves toggling between being a therapist and a facilitator. Whatever course of action is required—and coaches know their PLCs better than anyone—it is imperative that, however uncomfortable, they should address all conflicts and never dismiss them in hopes that they go away by the time of the next meeting. This almost never happens without addressing them and taking them head on. Even a partial resolution announces that *We put things on the table here.* Dispelling hard feelings then becomes of greater importance to the coach than bridging divergent opinions. When conflicts are resolved, coaches can rest easy that the PLC will become stronger for it, down the road if not by the time of the next meeting.

Pushing the Conversation Deeper

Like water, PLCs as a group tend to follow the path of least resistance. There is less resistance by teachers in agreeing with the majority opinion than disagreeing, in offering only suggestions rather than cool feedback, in affirming a colleague's work than respectfully pointing out gaps, and in silently noticing violations of group norms rather than actually calling a colleague on them.

While it is the shared responsibility of all PLC members to do the "hard stuff," it is fundamentally the job of the PLC coach to encourage the hard stuff, remind members of it, nurture it, and model it at every opportunity. On this note, coaches may never rest. Coaches keep a keen eye out for that opportunity to ask a member who has offered an opinion to clarify her thinking, or ask another, "What evidence do you see of that in the work?" A coach must embrace his role as the driving force that pushes teachers to go deeper, think harder, and not let anyone off the hook, including himself. Complacency and cordiality are often the primary impediments to substance and growth. In a perfect world, a PLC will collectively keep all conversations at an appropriately deep level; in reality, the *depth of discourse* graph will drop on its own from time to time. When it does, the coach must step up to the plate and guide the PLC back to the hard stuff. It is rarely the most popular thing to do, but it is nearly always the best thing to do. The following suggestions can help coaches push the conversation deeper:

Refocus the PLC on student learning and what is best for students.

Model by example what it means to push the conversation deeper.

Ask the hard questions (e.g., *Tell me why you think that? How will this help students? How does this align to the standards?*).

Publicly recognize and affirm others who ask hard questions.

Have members evaluate their PLC using the *High Functioning PLC Continuum* (see the Coach's Appendix).

Read and discuss recent professional literature.

Add a group norm related to *depth of discourse* when reviewing and updating group norms (e.g., *Ask one another the hard questions.* Or, simply *Go deep*).

Be open and honest when recent discussions are lacking depth. Frame your comments by stating something such as this: *I've noticed as of late our conversations are hitting on the surface of some important issues. How can I, as coach, help us dig deeper into what lies beneath the surface so that we can have a greater impact on student learning?* Above all, refrain from saying "you" or "you all" and say "we," "our," and "us" in discussing how things are going.

Rochelle Herring Peniston, president of the educational consulting firm Transformation by Design, has shared with me an apt comparison. A few years back, in an attempt to reduce the threat of terrorism in New York City, a campaign was initiated by the Metropolitan Transportation Authority to encourage subway patrons to speak up if they witnessed any suspicious behavior. Posters were hung in all subway trains and stations that announced the following: "If you see something, say something." This is a perfect credo for PLCs as they look at student and teacher work, examine data, and review team-designed CFAs. It is easier to be quiet and agreeable, but it is never better to do so when our intuition tells us that something has gaps or could be improved. **There is learning in the balance**. Each member of the PLC has the obligation to say something if she sees it. Our kids' learning is more important than the temporary discomfort we may feel in bringing to light issues and observations that, however unpopular, need addressing. I suggest PLC members sign and comply with the following Code of Discourse (see Figure 7.1):

Figure 7.1   PLC Members' Code of Discourse

1. Be honest.
2. Be respectful.
3. Dare to disagree.
4. Put kids first.
5. Don't take comments personally.
6. Don't offer comments personally.
7. Celebrate successes.
8. Don't be stubborn.
9. Trust the process.
10. If you see something, say something.
11. Leave your ego at the door, but bring your brains inside.

Sustaining the Momentum

In many ways, PLCs are living, breathing organisms. They are constantly evolving and growing and at times redefining themselves. As they become more seasoned and more familiar with the routines of engaging in the three Essential Tasks discussed in Part II of this book, they can often reach plateaus in their development. These plateaus are not an altogether bad thing; they are part of the process of maturing into a high functioning PLC.

During these times, it is the responsibility of the coach to keep the PLC from stagnating or merely going through the motions. To help sustain the excitement and momentum that PLCs experience during growth spurts, coaches can do some or all of the following:

Revisit with the PLC the purpose and goals of the PLC.

Revisit with the PLC the group norms, possibly updating them.

Revisit with the PLC the Code of Discourse.

Engage the PLC in a text-based discussion (using chapters contained herein or current educational articles).

Pass the facilitation on to another member for the next month of meetings.

Vary the focus (e.g., if the PLC has been looking at a lot of student work lately, focus on data or peer observations for a few meetings).

Arrange for the PLC to observe another PLC in the school.

This last suggestion can be surprisingly rejuvenating. An appealing feature of this is that the PLC observed need not be one that is further along than the PLC doing the observing. It really works well either way. If the PLC being observed is quite seasoned and doing most things well, then the observing PLC can meet later to debrief with the coach and ask the following: *What did you see? What did they do particularly well that we could do?* A useful discussion will likely result. If, on the other hand, the observed PLC is less high functioning, the experience is just as rich for those observing. The observing PLC can later debrief and ask the following: *What did you see? What would you recommend to this PLC?* Of course, the purpose is never to "fix" the PLC observed, and no feedback should be offered to members, but the act of thinking and discussing what *they* might need breathes new life into the observing PLC. Regardless of whether the PLC is ahead or behind, observing another PLC can help jump-start a PLC that has hit a plateau and spark continued growth.

Retooling Existing Ineffective PLCs

I recall being invited to one school to visit a seventh-grade math PLC during one of the PLC meetings. My charge was to help them become a more collaborative team. There were seven teachers on the team, led by a designated PLC team leader. They met every other day at tables in the school's Media Center. The first thing I noticed was the seven teachers occupied five different tables in the Media Center! Only half of the teachers actually sat facing the team leader, who did her best to lead the meeting. Two of the teachers graded papers and a third worked on her laptop on some student action plan that was due. There was no collaboration, no unity, no cohesive focus. Yet they called themselves the Math 7 PLC.

As I have mentioned throughout this book, the recent popularity of PLCs has given rise to all kinds of teacher groups that bear the PLC title but in practice lack PLC authenticity. It's easy to give a group the name "PLC," but it is much more difficult to actually do the hard work of an authentic PLC. Some schools realize this. These schools and districts that recognize this disconnect must retool their existing teacher groups to become authentic PLCs.

Refocusing existing PLCs to collaborate on authentic tasks takes work. It requires replacing old habits with new ones, replacing an existing culture of noncollaboration (or superficial collaboration) with a new culture in which teachers are dependent on one another, openly but respectfully critical of one another, and keenly focused on student success.

Principals are at the helm in retooling existing, wayward PLCs. There is no getting around this truth. There is only so much an ineffective PLC can do on its own to change its paradigm and existing habits. Principals who expect their PLCs to become effective after sending admonishing emails or announcing their desires for change at staff meetings are likely to be as ineffective as their faculties' PLCs.

A NOTE TO PRINCIPALS

To achieve this shift in habits, PLCs must have strong administrative support. School principals must be clear about the changes they expect in existing PLCs and be transparent in leading their faculties during the transition year from "teacher groups" to "authentic PLCs." This shift will require principals to expend deliberate energy and time and, if it is to happen with fidelity, making the shift a reality must top the principals' priority list. Nothing less will work. If principals decide that their existing PLCs are ineffective in their present form, it may be necessary to restructure the teams, particularly the leadership of the PLCs.

Change and Train the Coach

In most cases, teachers who lead existing nonauthentic PLCs are *de facto* leaders—often department chairs or grade-level lead teachers who existed as team leaders before the school decided to have PLCs. As such, they are very often not the best choice for PLC coaches, as per the criteria identified in Table 2.1. They are usually veteran teachers who have been at the school the longest and have been appointed by principals in part due to their long-standing relationships with those principals. That doesn't make them poor choices as PLC coaches per se, but in many cases they simply lack the skills needed to lead an authentic PLC. And in some cases, these teachers may not be interested in obtaining those skills.

For these reasons, school administrators need to revisit the criteria in Table 2.1 and select a new coach on that basis. If, after doing so, an existing leader remains the best choice for coach, then so be it. But more than likely, a new candidate for coach will emerge. Regardless if an existing leader maintains his leadership role or if a new teacher is selected to take it on, the new coach will need to be trained or otherwise become knowledgeable in coaching an authentic PLC. This can happen by having new coaches study the contents of this or other books on the subject of facilitating PLCs or by attending the PLC Coaches Summer Institute offered each year by the Center for Authentic PLCs (for information on the Institute, go to www.authenticPLCs.com).

It is essential that coaches acquire adequate knowledge and training to lead a PLC, because the effectiveness of the PLC depends on the effectiveness of the coach who leads it.

In addition to visible administrative support and changing the PLC leadership, the PLC itself can do the following:

Change the Physical Environment

The first thing a teacher does in stepping up the management of a way-ward class of students is to change their seating arrangement. As every classroom teacher knows, changing the seating assignments of students helps change the students' mentality. It is a constant visible reminder: *That was then* (old seating assignments, old classroom procedures and expectations); *this is now* (new seating assignments, new classroom procedures and expectations).

PLCs wishing to change course in what they do and, most importantly, how they do it, would be well advised to change the physical environment in which they meet. Of course, if the role of facilitator has shifted to a new teacher in the PLC, it makes sense that the room in which the PLC meets will also change (to the room of the teacher now leading the group). Additionally, the seating arrangement of the team should also change. If teachers are used to sitting in a scattered arrangement, now is the time to have folks sit together—ideally, in a circle, facing one another—in a man-ner conducive to true collaboration. If we want teachers to behave as a collaborative team, it's time to sit as a collaborative team. There is more to this than meets the eye. I can often assess the degree of collaboration of a PLC just by observing how teachers sit together (or not) in the room in which they meet.

Start With Team Building

For all the reasons emphasized in Chapter 2, team building and norm setting act as vital building blocks in becoming an authentic PLC. It's not too late to engage an existing PLC in these pursuits. Team building pro-vides the very ingredient that may have been lacking in the original pseudo-PLC. So long as the team remains a simple collection of individual teachers and fails to be a cohesive entity onto its own, the team is not likely to be or act as an authentic PLC. The shift from a "group of teachers" to an "interdependent team of teachers" begins with team building and norm setting (see Chapter 2 for how to do these things effectively). It may seem a bit odd to engage in these activities with a preexisting team, but what members stand to learn about each other during *Traffic Jam, Compass Points,* and *Peeves & Traits Protocol* will prove to be worth the time invested.

Then Do a Book Study

Before an ineffective PLC can transition to become an authentic PLC, members need to learn about authentic PLCs. The fastest and easiest way to facilitate this learning is for the PLC to designate several meetings to discuss what authentic PLCs do and how they do it. Using the *Text-Based Discussion* or *Final Word* protocols to engage members with the text helps to keep the discussion focused and scholarly, unites teachers as a team, and provides important experiences using protocols. As teachers begin to understand their new roles in an authentic PLC, they are constructing community knowledge together. (I admit my personal bias, but *The Practice of Authentic PLCs* is a great resource to consider using.)

Next Do a Self-Assessment

Each of the aforementioned endeavors helps lay the necessary groundwork required to move existing PLCs toward authenticity. One way for teams to assess where they are along the way to PLC authenticity is for members to gauge themselves against the *High Functioning PLC Continuum* in the Coach's Appendix.

By honestly looking at where they are in terms of collaboration, existing PLCs—no matter how divergent they may be from the goal of authenticity—can begin to set goals and take steps to "authenticate" their teams. In the case of the Math 7 PLC, a discussion can begin by reading about authentic PLCs. This can lead teachers to conclude the following: *Maybe we can do this better. Maybe we can shoot for some characteristics more closely aligned to the PLC ideal* (such as those mentioned in the *High Functioning PLC Continuum).* At the very least, rearranging their physical environment and sitting at a single table, facing one another, would help propel group members toward the goal of working collaboratively to examine and improve student learning.

Authenticating established PLCs requires fundamental shifts in the tasks in which the team engages, how team members engage in those tasks, how they work together in a truly collaborative way, and in the roles that are embraced by members. Additionally, principals must make PLC authenticity a high priority and impress upon their faculties the goal of their PLCs: In the short term, the goal is to retool the structure and functions of the team, and in the long term, the goal is to have a real impact on student learning.

SUMMARY: COACHING TEACHERS

Coaching an authentic PLC, complete with the frustrations and challenges such teams present, is among the most personally and professionally rewarding experiences a teacher leader can do for her school. With each problem solved, each bit of student or teacher work examined and improved, each revelation brought to the surface by digging deeply into data, the PLC moves closer to making great strides in improving student learning. There are many small successes along the way to greatness and it is the unrelenting pursuit of these successes by a determined and sensitive coach that permits the sum of these successes to amount to observable gains for students.

Dealing with difficult team dynamics is never easy or fun, but coaches must address conflicts as they inevitably arise so that their teams can move forward effectively. Coaches must also deal productively with reluctant members and realize that these members require different strategies than resistant teachers.

Coaches should reflect often on the Code of Discourse and use the *High Functioning PLC Continuum* to assess where their teams are along the journey to authentic collaboration. Maintenance is key; it is never enough for coaches to be complacent that their teams are high functioning without checking periodically to make sure the graphs haven't dropped.

PLCs depend on trust, and coaches must trust that their members will rise to the standards and challenges with which they are presented. Periodically passing on the facilitation role to other members requires readiness on the part of the new facilitator and trust on the part of the coach. Others teachers on the team can lead the PLC through important conversations and experiences. Coaching an authentic PLC is a privilege, and what challenges arise are few in number when compared to the rewards of leading a team toward significant improvement in the learning of the PLC's students.

COACH'S APPENDIX

High Functioning PLC Continuum

Written in collaboration with Cari Begin.

Purpose and Vision

FOCUS

Low Functioning → *High Functioning*

Low Functioning	High Functioning
Multiple foci detract from central purpose; individual teacher agendas derail focus; no unified vision	Clear focus on student learning; members have common vision of what to do and how to accomplish goals

Interpersonal Dynamics

TRUST

Low Functioning → *High Functioning*

Low Functioning	High Functioning
Significant distrust; members are unwilling to be vulnerable or take risks	High trust level; members show willingness to be vulnerable

HONESTY IN DISCOURSE

Low Functioning → *High Functioning*

Low Functioning	High Functioning
Superficial discourse is the rule; celebration is valued over critical analysis; members are reluctant to be candid	Members speak honestly and openly; show comfort in getting concerns out in the open

	Low Functioning	High Functioning
INTERDEPENDENCE	No member dependence; pockets of allies exist for personal gain; several members wou'd prefer to work alone	Members clearly depend on PLC for improvement, believing their work is better for it
GROUP NORMS	No norms have been formalized in writing, or if so, norms are never really followed or referred to again (after their creation)	Norms are followed w/minor exceptions; norms are reviewed, updated, and policed by all
CONFLICT RESOLUTION	Ill feelings are not addressed and hamper progress of the group	All conflicts are addressed until parties involved achieve resolution
HANDLING OF DISAGREEMENT	Members outwardly agree; disagreements are seen as negative and therefore avoided	Differing opinions are embraced w/all voices validated and heard

(Continued)

PERSONAL COMMITMENT

Low Functioning → *High Functioning*

Low Functioning	High Functioning
General lack of commitment to the concept of PLC and to the work; apathy is the rule; compliance overshadows commitment; skepticism and resentment exist w/some members	All members demonstrate commitment to purpose and goals and take personal responsibility for the work; members hold each other to high standards of commitment

DEPTH OF DISCOURSE

Low Functioning → *High Functioning*

Low Functioning	High Functioning
Discourse is superficial; members go through the motions w/little or no thoughtfulness; conversations dominated by individual teacher agendas	Digging deep into issues is the rule; members hold each other to a high standard of thoughtfulness

Engagement in the Work

LOOKING AT TEACHER WORK AND ISSUES

Low Functioning → *High Functioning*

Low Functioning	High Functioning
Teacher work is rarely shared, and if so, a "show and tell" model is used with little or no feedback	Teacher work is shared often and meaningful feedback is given; work is always modified based on the feedback; protocols are used routinely

LOOKING AT STUDENT WORK

Low Functioning → *High Functioning*

Low Functioning	High Functioning
Teacher discussions are rarely accompanied by student work, and if they are, nothing is addressed to make the work better in significant ways	Student work is examined frequently with the use of protocols; learning gaps, alignment to ELOs and degree of rigor are common foci

	Low Functioning	High Functioning
DESIGNING CFAs (Common Formative Assessments)	Assessments are not written together, or if they are, individual teachers write separate components without team significant feedback or modification; scoring schema are inconsistent across team; assessments are written during or after instruction	All members design all components of each assessment; CFAs are created prior to instruction and are organized by ELOs with scoring criteria for mastery; multiple choice items comprise a small percentage of items
REVIEWING DATA	Data are used to excuse ineffective teaching by placing blame on external factors; cursory review of broad, summative data is the extent of data usage	Teachers have frequent, blame-free discussions of student data, moving from *macrodata to microdata (including student work samples)*; the pursuit of additional data is driven by Exploratory Questions that identify a *problem of practice*
RESPONDING TO DATA	No plans are designed for students who don't learn, or if they are, plans consist of repeating ineffective methods that were used originally	The data inform both instructional decisions and plans of action for students who fail to master learning objectives these are decided before instruction begins and are regularly assessed for effectiveness using new data
PEER OBSERVATIONS	No peer observations occur	Members are comfortable with peer visitors and observe each other periodically; visits are debriefed using protocols

(Continued)

(Continued)

Facilitation

PROFESSIONAL LEARNING

Low Functioning →

Teachers are complacent with existing knowledge and ways of doing things; learning new ideas is not a pursuit of the team (though it may be for individual teachers)

High Functioning →

Teachers are continually engaging with new knowledge from each other and from other professional sources; constructing knowledge as a community is routine; risk-taking is practiced and encouraged

MEETING LOGISTICS

Low Functioning →

Inconsistent meeting start and end times; teachers sit scattered around the room; no clear agenda; environment contains many distractions; meetings lack focus and purpose

High Functioning →

Meetings start and end on time; teachers sit together facing one another; agendas are clear; environment is conducive to maintaining focus and keep distractions to a minimum

ATTENTION TO TEAM DYNAMICS

Low Functioning →

Coach is unaware or unresponsive to the team's interpersonal dynamics

High Functioning →

Coach skillfully balances individual needs with the group's needs; coach addresses interpersonal issues and deals with them effectively; coach ensures all members have voice

DEPTH OF DISCOURSE

Low Functioning

Coach neglects to ask the hard questions or push members to abide by the *Code of Discourse*; discussions are superficial

High Functioning

Coach pushes members to abide by the *Code of Discourse*

ACCOUNTABILITY

Low Functioning

Little or no accountability exists; coach fails to hold members to a high level of commitment; excuses are commonplace and accepted by the coach without question

High Functioning

Coach holds self and members to high standards of accountability for being fully engaged in the work, during and between meetings

Administrative Support

PRIORITY

Low Functioning

Administrators may extol their value of PLCs, but their actions demonstrate little priority to the work

High Functioning

Actions of administrators demonstrate that PLCs are a high priority

145

PLC Members' Code of Discourse

1. Be honest.

2. Be respectful.

3. Dare to disagree.

4. Put kids first.

5. Don't take comments personally.

6. Don't offer comments personally.

7. Celebrate successes.

8. Don't be stubborn.

9. Trust the process.

10. If you see something, say something.

11. Leave your ego at the door, but bring your brains inside.

Suggested First-Year Timeline for CPLCs and PLCs

The following timeline assumes PLCs will meet at least weekly,
each time for no less than 60 minutes. Protocols are listed in italics.

Month	Primary Focus of CPLC	Primary Focus of PLCs
June	• Principal and assistant principals read *The Practice of Authentic PLCs* • Principal establishes PLC teams and selects coaches (refer to Chapter 2)	None
July	• Principal and coaches attend *PLC Coaches Summer Institute* for training	• Faculty summer reading: *The Practice of Authentic PLCs* (Chapter 1)
August	• Team building: *Traffic Jam, Inquiring Introductions* • Set norms: *Compass Points, Peeves & Traits, Norm-Setting Protocol* • Text-based discussion: *The Practice of Authentic PLCs* (Chapter 6)	• Team building: *Traffic Jam, Inquiring Introductions* • Text-based discussion: *On Common Ground* (Chapter 3)
September	• Text-based discussion: *The Practice of Authentic PLCs* (Chapter 3) • View *Tuning Protocol* video (ASCD, SMS) • *Notice & Wonder*—Student Work* • *Tuning Protocol*—Student Work* • *Tuning Protocol*—Teacher Work*	• Set norms: *Compass Points, Peeves & Traits, Norm-Setting Protocol* • Text-based discussion: *The Practice of Authentic PLCs* (Chapter 2, Deciding ELOs; Chapter 4, Deciding Assessment Content) • Decide Essential Learning Outcomes • Unpack the standards
October	• Text-based discussion: *The Practice of Authentic PLCs* (Chapter 4) • *Consultancy Protocol*—Teacher Work* • *Charette Protocol*—Teacher Work* • *Hopes & Fears* Protocol • Review *High Functioning PLC Continuum* (refer to Coach's Appendix)	• Text-based discussion: *The Practice of Authentic PLCs* (Chapter 3) • Review and sign *PLC Members' Code of Discourse* (refer to Coach's Appendix) • View *Tuning Protocol* video (ASCD, SMS) • *Notice & Wonder*—Student Work* • *Tuning Protocol*—Student Work*

(Continued)

(Continued)

November	• Plan logistics for peer observations (refer to Chapter 2) • Text-based discussion: *The Practice of Authentic PLCs* (Chapter 5) • *Notice & Wonder*—Data	• Text-based discussion: *The Practice of Authentic PLCs* (Chapter 4) • Begin peer observations (including a PLC meeting to debrief) • *Tuning Protocol*— Teacher Work* • *Consultancy Protocol*— Teacher Work*
December	• Text-based discussion: *The Practice of Authentic PLCs* (Chapter 7) • Self-evaluate using *High Functioning PLC Continuum* (refer to Coach's Appendix)	• Text-based discussion: *The Practice of Authentic PLCs* (Chapter 5) • *Notice & Wonder*—Data • Self-evaluate using *High Functioning PLC Continuum* (refer to Coach's Appendix)
January–April	• Collaborate on ways to assist individual PLCs with designing quality CFAs and responding appropriately to data	• (January) Discuss and update forms • Focus on designing CFAs and responding to data (refer to Chapters 4 & 5) • Continue using protocols to look at teacher and student work (add the *Charette Protocol*) • Continue peer observations
May	• Continue to discuss progress of individual PLCs, troubleshoot issues with protocols • Continue engaging in text-based discussions	• Focus on using data to structure EOC review and identify Tier 2 and 3 students (refer to Chapter 4, *Response to Intervention*)
June	• Debrief year using *High Functioning PLC Continuum* (refer to Coach's Appendix) • Decide plan of action for training new coaches for next year	• Debrief year using *High Functioning PLC Continuum* (refer to Coach's Appendix)

*It is imperative that work brought for examination must be a coach's own work (or the work of her students), not the work from a member of her PLC. Bringing work from a colleague, rather than one's own work, completely changes the dynamic of the feedback.

PROTOCOLS AND ACTIVITIES

Traffic Jam

Compass Points

Peeves & Traits Protocol

Norm-Setting Protocol

Text-Based Seminar Guidelines

Final Word Protocol

Notice & Wonder Protocol—Student Work

Notice & Wonder Protocol—Data

Tuning Protocol

Consultancy Protocol

Consultancy Protocol—Student Work

Charette Protocol

Hopes & Fears Protocol

Inquiring Introductions Protocol

Examining Assessments

Peeling the Onion: Developing a Problem Protocol

Passion Profiles Activity

Passion Profiles

Traffic Jam

A team–building activity that mirrors the characteristics of a PLC.

Time allotted: 45 minutes (25 minutes for task, 20 minutes for debrief/ discussion)

Materials: 7 mouse pads, cardstock paper, or masking tape to mark off the "stones"

Participants: 6 volunteers

There are seven stepping stones placed on the floor in a line, with spaces between them. On the three left-hand stones, facing right, stand three of the people. The other three people stand on the three right-hand stones, and face left. The center stone is not occupied to start.

The challenge: exchanging places

Participants move so that the people originally standing on the right-hand stepping stones end up on the left-hand stones, and those originally standing on the left-hand stepping stones end up on the right-hand stones, with the center stone again unoccupied.

The rules:

- After each move, each person must be standing on a stepping stone.
- Participants may only move forward, in the direction they originally face.
- There are two ways to move forward:
  - Participants may *jump* one person if there is an empty stone on the other side. Only one person may be *jumped,* and that person must be facing the *jumper.* (i.e., someone from the other side of three).
  - Participants may *slide* to an empty stone directly in front of them.

- If the group finds itself in a "traffic jam," participants must go *all the way back* to the starting position and try again. They may *not* simply redo the last few moves.

Compass Points

An exercise in understanding preferences in group work.
Developed in the field by educators affiliated
with the National School Reform Faculty (NSRF).

Time: 35 minutes

1. The room is divided into four sections: North, South, East, and West.

2. PLC members are asked to place themselves at one of the four stations based on their style in working as part of a group (see below). It is worth noting that most teachers see themselves as some combination of these four; they should nonetheless commit to one that is most dominant in their style. (3 minutes)

North
Acting–"Let's do it."
Likes to act, try things, plunge in

West
Attention to Detail–Likes
to know the who, what,
when, where and how
before acting

East
Speculating–Likes to
look at the big picture and
possibilities before acting

South
Feeling–Likes to know that everyone's
feelings have been taken into
consideration and that their voices have
been heard before acting

3. At each Compass Point, the teachers answer the following and post their group responses on chart paper. (20 minutes)

   a. List three strengths of your style.

   b. List three limitations of your style.

   c. Which style do you find most difficult to work with and why?

   d. What do people from other styles need to know about you so you can work together effectively?

   e. What do you value about each of the other three styles?

4. The group of teachers at each Compass Point shares out to the large group. (12 minutes)

Peeves & Traits Protocol

Time: 20 minutes

1. Participants are each given an index card (5″ × 7″).

2. On one side of the card, participants write down *one* pet peeve they have regarding working in groups or at teacher meetings. They begin their pet peeve with the following phrase:

"It burns my butt when . . ."

(e.g., *"It burns my butt when people come late to meetings,"* or *"It burns my butt when people are interrupted during discussions,"* or *"It burns my butt when one person does all the talking,"* etc.) (5 minutes)

3. On the other side of the card, participants write *one* trait about themselves that everyone in the group should know about them in order to work best with them in a group setting. They begin their trait with the following phrase:

"One thing you all should know about me is . . ."

(e.g., *"One thing you all should know about me is that my silence is not due to disinterest; I just need process time,"* or *"One thing you all should know about me is I get excited during discussions and sometimes people are put off by my enthusiasm,"* or *"One thing you all should know about me is I am very visual and need to see on chart paper or on the Smart Board what we're discussing,"* etc.) (5 minutes)

4. Participants share both sides of their card in volunteer order without discussion (or elaborating on the card). (10 minutes)

Norm-Setting Protocol

Time: 60 minutes

1. The coach gives participants three index cards (5" × 7") and a black marker.

2. Writing on only one side of the card, participants write down *one* group norm they would like to see. No more than one norm per card; participants can write as many cards as they like. (5 minutes)

3. The coach collects all cards and randomly passes them out to participants. Each participant reads the cards she has been given and other participants share their card if theirs is the same or closely related to the one being read. As cards are read, they are collected by the facilitator and posted in groups of like norms (e.g., "respect," "disagreements," "agenda," etc.). Discussion is limited to grouping norms and identifying similarities between norms. (20 minutes)

4. *Dissent option.* After the coach posts all cards into categories (though some will be "stand alones"), participants can propose to eliminate any norm. If one other participant "seconds" the opinion that a particular norm be eliminated, the index card of that norm is removed. (5 minutes)

5. As a whole group, the facilitator leads a discussion of condensing each group of norms into a single norm (without stringing them all together with the use of "and"). The goal is to word a single norm that captures the essence of the group of like norms. (30 minutes)

6. *Next steps.* The facilitator asks for a volunteer to do whatever "word-smithing" is still needed for the norms, after the meeting. The final product is a list of four to six group norms that will govern all discourse in the PLC. [I like to make a poster of the final list and have all PLC members sign the poster. It is then displayed prominently in the meeting room.] Hereafter, the group norms should appear at the bottom of each meeting agenda.

Text-Based Seminar Guidelines

Developed by Gene Thompson-Grove.

Purpose: Enlargement of understanding a text, *not* the achievement of some particular understanding.

Ground Rules:

- Refer to the text, and challenge others to go to the text. Use page numbers. Wait for others to get to the quote, then read it aloud.
- Listen actively.
- Build on what others say, referring to them by name.
- Don't step on others' talk. Allow for silences and pauses. Make time and space so everyone can participate.
- Converse directly with each other, and let the conversation flow as much as possible—without raising hands or using a speaker's list.
- Make the assumptions underlying your comments explicit to others.
- Ask questions of others in order to build understanding.

Final Word Protocol

Developed by Jennifer Fischer-Mueller and Gene Thompson-Grove for the NSRF.

Purpose: The purpose of this discussion format is to give each person in the group an opportunity to have their ideas, understanding, and perspective enhanced by hearing from others. With this format, the group can explore an article, clarify their thinking, and have their assumptions and beliefs questioned in order to gain a deeper understanding of the issue.

Roles: Facilitator/timekeeper (who also participates); participants

Facilitation: Have participants identify one "most" significant idea from the test (underlined or highlighted ahead of time), stick to the time limits, avoid dialogue, have equal sized circles so all small groups finish at approximately the same time.

Process:

1. Sit in a circle, and identify a facilitator/timekeeper.

2. Each person needs to have one "most" significant idea from the test underlined or highlighted in the article. It is often helpful to identify a "back up" quote as well.

3. The first person begins by reading what "struck him or her the most" from the article. Have this person refer to where the quote is in the text—one thought or quote only. Then, in less than 3 minutes, this person describes why that quote struck him or her. For example, why does s/he agree/disagree with the quote, what questions does s/he have about the quote, what issues does it raise for him or her, what does s/he now wonder about in relation to that quote?

4. Continuing around the circle, each person responds to that quote and what the presenter said, briefly, in less than a minute. The purpose of the response is

to expand on the presenter's thinking about the quote and the issues raised for him or her by the quote,

to provide a different look at the quote,

to clarify the presenter's thinking about the quote, and/or

to question the presenter's assumptions about the quote and the issues raised (although at this time there is no response from the presenter).

5. After going around the circle with each person having responded for less than 1 minute, the person who began has the "final word." In no more than 1 minute the presenter responds to what has been said. Now what is s/he thinking? What is his or her reaction to what s/he has heard?

6. The next person in the circle then begins by sharing what struck him or her most from the next. Proceed around the circle, responding to this next presenter's quote in the same way as the first presenter's. This process continues until each person has had a round with his or her quote.

7. For each round, allow about 8 minutes (circles of five participants: presenter 3 minutes, response 1 minute for four people, final word for presenter 1 minute). The role of the facilitator is to keep the process moving, keep it clear and directed to the article, and keep time so everyone gets an opportunity for a round. Total time is about 40 minutes for a group of five (32 minutes for a group of four, 48 minutes for a group of six). End by debriefing the process in your small group.

Notice & Wonder Protocol—Student Work

A protocol for analyzing and discussing student work

Time: 45 minutes

1. Participants are presented with a sample of student work pertaining to their practice. This might be a single piece of work from one student copied for all participants or class samples of the same assignment, with each participant getting an individual student's work. It generally provides richer discussion if the work is corrected or scored by the presenting teacher.

2. The presenter of the work briefly provides the context in which the work was assigned (e.g., grade level of students, description of the unit on which the students were working, prior knowledge of students, how long the students were given to complete the work, etc.). *Participants are silent and take notes.* (5 minutes)

3. The participants ask clarifying questions of the presenter. These are questions that provide information that participants feel they need to better understand the context. The presenter answers each clarifying question briefly, in a sentence or two. (5 minutes)

4. Each participant is given a 5″ × 7″ index card. Quietly and individually, participants write three observations evident in the work sample. These observations must be free of inference or speculation; they are factually based from objectively examining the work sample. Each observation starts with the phrase, "*I notice that. . . .*" (5 minutes)

5. *Round 1.* In turn, each participant reads aloud one new observation that has not yet been shared, each time beginning with the phrase, "*I notice that . . . .*" After the last participant shares one new observation, the first participant offers a second new observation and the process continues until all observations have been shared aloud, *without discussion. The presenter is quiet and takes notes.* (5 minutes)

6. Each participant turns over his index card and quietly writes three suggestions or question-statements based on any observations heard in Round 1. These comments attempt to offer possible suggestions or pose questions for the presenter to think about. No attempt should be made to *evaluate* the work or the assignment; the intent is for the presenter to gain insights into how to strengthen the assignment or the method used to score the assignment. Each comment starts with the phrase, "*I wonder if . . . .*" (5 minutes)

7. *Round 2.* In turn, each participant reads aloud one new thought that has not yet been shared, each time beginning with the phrase, "*I wonder . . . .*" This process continues as in Round 1 until all speculations have

been shared aloud, *without discussion. The presenter is quiet and takes notes.* (10 minutes)

8. *Reflection.* The presenter quietly reviews her notes and then reflects aloud to the group any thoughts related to the comments she heard. *The participants are silent.* (5 minutes)

9. *Debrief.* The team now debriefs the *process* and refrains from additional comments pertaining to the student work samples. (5 minutes)

Notice & Wonder Protocol—Data

A protocol for analyzing data both descriptively and inferentially.

Time: 40 minutes

1. Participants are presented with a table and/or graph of data pertaining to their practice. The data set may be displayed on a screen for all to see, or it may be given to each PLC member in hardcopy form. (I prefer the former, since graphs and sometimes data in table form are often illustrated in color.)

2. Each participant is given a 5″ × 7″ index card. Quietly and individually, participants write three observations evident in the graph or table. These observations must be free of inference or speculation; they are factually based from objectively examining the display. Each observation starts with the phrase, *"I notice that. . . ."* (5 minutes)

3. *Round 1.* In turn, each participant reads aloud one new observation that has not yet been shared, each time beginning with the phrase, *"I notice that. . . ."* The facilitator records the responses on chart paper. After the last participant shares one new observation, the first participant offers a second new observation and the process continues until all observations have been shared aloud, *without discussion.* (5 minutes)

4. Each participant turns over his index card and quietly writes three speculations or question-statements based on the observations heard in Round 1. These speculations attempt to offer possible explanations for the observations or pose suggestions for pursuing additional data. No attempt should be made to *solve* the problems that surface; the intent is to gain insights into what the data suggest, how the data are connected, and what the data imply. Each speculation starts with the phrase, *"I wonder why. . . ."* or *"I wonder if. . . ."* (5 minutes)

5. *Round 2.* In turn, each participant reads aloud one new speculation that has not yet been shared, each time beginning with the phrase, *"I wonder. . . ."* The facilitator records the responses on chart paper. This process continues as in Round 1 until all speculations have been shared aloud, *without discussion.* (10 minutes)

6. *Discussion.* PLC members discuss what has been shared and possible causes, connections, and links to classroom instruction and note other additional data that may be needed. (15 minutes)

Tuning Protocol

Developed by Joseph McDonald and David Allen.

1. Introduction (5 minutes)
   - Facilitator briefly introduces protocol goals, guidelines, and schedule
   - Participants briefly introduce themselves (if necessary)

2. Presentation (15 minutes)
   The presenter has an opportunity to share the context for the student work:

   - Information about the students and/or the class—what the students tend to be like, where they are in school, where they are in the year
   - Assignment or prompt that generated the student work
   - Student learning goals or standards that inform the work
   - Samples of student work—photocopies of work, video clips, etc.—with student names removed
   - Evaluation format—scoring rubric and/or assessment criteria, etc.
   - Focusing question for feedback
   - Participants are silent; no questions are entertained at this time

3. Clarifying Questions (5 minutes)
   - Participants have an opportunity to ask "clarifying" questions in order to get information that may have been omitted in the presentation that they feel would help them to understand the context for the student work. Clarifying questions are matters of "fact."
   - The facilitator should be sure to limit the questions to those that are "clarifying," judging which questions more properly belong in the warm/cool feedback section.

4. Examination of Student Work Samples (15 minutes)
   - Participants look closely at the work, taking notes on where it seems to be in tune with the stated goals, and where there might be a problem. Participants focus particularly on the presenter's focusing question.
   - Presenter is silent; participants do this work silently.

5. Pause to reflect on warm and cool feedback (2–3 minutes)
   - Participants take a couple of minutes to reflect on what they would like to contribute to the feedback session.
   - Presenter is silent; participants do this work silently.

6. Warm and Cool Feedback (15 minutes)
   - Participants share feedback with each other while the presenter is silent. The feedback generally begins with a few minutes of warm feedback, moves on to a few minutes of cool feedback (sometimes phrased in the form of reflective questions), and then moves back and forth between warm and cool feedback.

- Warm feedback may include comments about how the work presented seems to meet the desired goals; cool feedback may include possible "disconnects," gaps, or problems. Often participants offer ideas or suggestions for strengthening the work presented.
- The facilitator may need to remind participants of the presenter's focusing question, which should be posted for all to see.
- Presenter is silent and takes notes.

7. Reflection (5 minutes)
   - Presenter speaks to those comments/questions he or she chooses while participants are silent.
   - This is not a time to defend oneself, but is instead a time for the presenter to reflect aloud on those ideas or questions that seemed particularly interesting.
   - Facilitator may intervene to focus, clarify, etc.

8. Debrief (5 minutes)
   - Facilitator-led discussion of this tuning experience.

Consultancy Protocol

The Consultancy Protocol was developed by
Gene Thompson–Grove, Paula Evans, and Faith Dunne as part of the
Coalition of Essential Schools' National Re:Learning Faculty Program,
and further adapted and revised as part of the work of NSRF.

A consultancy is a structured process for helping an individual or a team think more expansively about a particular, concrete dilemma.

Time: Approximately 50 minutes

Roles:

Presenter (whose work is being discussed by the group)

Facilitator (who sometimes participates, depending on the size of the group)

1. The presenter gives an overview of the dilemma with which s/he is struggling, and frames a question for the consultancy group to consider. The framing of this question, as well as the quality of the presenter's reflection on the dilemma being discussed, are key features of this protocol. If the presenter has brought student work, educator work, or other "artifacts," there is a pause here to silently examine the work/documents. The focus of the group's conversation is on the dilemma. (5–10 minutes).

2. The Consultancy group asks clarifying questions of the presenter—that is, questions that have brief, factual answers. (5 minutes)

3. The group asks probing questions of the presenter. These questions should be worked so that they help the presenter clarify and expand his/her thinking about the dilemma presented to the Consultancy group. The goal here is for the presenter to learn more about the question s/he framed or to do some analysis of the dilemma presented. The presenter may respond to the group's questions, but there is no discussion by the consultancy group of the presenter's responses. At the end of the 10 minutes, the facilitator asks the presenter to restate his/her question for the group. (10 minutes)

4. The group talks with each other about the dilemma presented. (15 minutes)

Possible questions to frame the discussion:

What did we hear?

What didn't we hear that we think might be relevant?

What assumptions seem to be operating?

What questions does the dilemma raise for us?

What do we think about the dilemma?

What might we do or try if faced with a similar dilemma? What have we done in similar situations?

Members of the group sometimes suggest actions the presenter might consider taking. Most often, however, they work to define the issues more thoroughly and objectively. The presenter doesn't speak during this discussion, but instead listens and takes notes.

5. The presenter reflects on what s/he heard and on what s/he is now thinking, sharing with the group anything that particularly resonated for him or her during any part of the Consultancy. (5 minutes)

6. The facilitator leads a brief conversation about the group's observation of the Consultancy process. (5 minutes)

Consultancy Protocol—Student Work

Adapted for examining student work.
Developed in the field by educators affiliated with NSRF.

Time: At least 1 hour

Roles:

Presenter (whose student is being discussed by the group)

Facilitator (who also participates)

Steps:

1. The presenter gives a quick overview of the student work. S/he highlights the major issues or concerns, and frames a question for the consultancy group to consider. The framing of this question, as well as the quality of the presenter's reflection on the student work and related issues, are key features of this protocol. (5 minutes)

2. The group examines the student work. (5 minutes)

3. The consultancy group asks clarifying questions of the presenter—that is, questions that have brief factual answers. (5 minutes)

4. The group asks probing questions of the presenter—these questions should be worded so that they help the presenter clarify and expand his or her thinking about the issue or question s/he raised for the consultancy group. The goal here is for the presenter to learn more about the question s/he framed or to do some analysis of the issue s/he presented. The presenter responds to the group's questions, but there is no discussion by the larger group of the presenter's responses. (10 minutes)

5. The group talks with each other about the student work and related issues in light of the questions framed for the group by the presenter. What did we hear? What didn't we hear that we needed to know more about? What do we think about the question and issue(s) presented?

Some groups like to begin the conversation with "warm" feedback—answering questions like, "What are the strengths in this situation or in this student's work?" or "What's the good news here?" The group then moves on to cooler feedback—answering questions like: "Where are the gaps?" "What isn't the presenter considering?" "What do areas for further improvement or investigation seem to be?" Sometimes the group will raise questions for the presenter to consider ("I wonder what would happen if . . . .?" or "I wonder why . . . ?"). The presenter is not allowed to speak during this discussion but instead listens and takes notes. (15 minutes)

6. The presenter responds to what s/he heard (first in a fishbowl if there are several presenters). A whole group discussion might then take place, depending on the time allotted. (10 minutes)

7. The facilitator leads a brief conversation about the group's observation of the process. (10 minutes)

Charette Protocol

Original written by Kathy Juarez, Piner High School, Santa Rosa, California.
Revised by Gene Thompson-Grove, January 2003, NSRF.
Revised by Kim Feicke, October 2007, NSRF.

The following list of steps attempts to formalize the process for others interested in using it.

1. A team or an individual requests a charette when

    a. the team/individual is experiencing difficulty with the work,

    b. a stopping point has been reached, or

    c. additional minds (thinkers new to the work) could help move it forward.

2. A group, ranging in size from three to six people, is formed to look at the work. A moderator/facilitator is designated from the newly formed group. It is the moderator's job to observe the charette, record information that is being created, ask questions along the way, and occasionally summarize the discussion.

3. The requesting team/individual presents its "work in progress" while the group listens. (There are no strict time limits, but this usually takes 5 or 10 minutes.) Sometimes, the invited group needs to ask two or three clarifying questions before moving on to step 4.

4. The requesting team/individual states what it needs or wants from the charette, thereby accepting responsibility for focusing the discussion. The focus is usually made in the form of a specific request, but it can be as generic as "How can we make this better?" or "What is our next step?"

5. The invited group then discusses while the requesting team/individual listens and takes notes. There are no hard and fast rules here. Occasionally (but not usually) the requesting team/individual joins in the discussion process. The emphasis is on improving the work, which now belongs to the entire group. The atmosphere is one of "we're in this together," and our single purpose is "to make a good thing even better."

6. When the requesting team/individual knows it has gotten what it needs from the invited group, they stop the process, briefly summarize what was gained, thank the participants and moderator and return to the "drawing board."

7. Debrief the process as a group.

Hopes & Fears Protocol

Modified from the version suggested in The Power of Protocols by McDonald, Mohr, Dichter, and McDonald (2007).

Time: 60 minutes

Purpose: To bring to light hopes and fears associated with trying something new that requires change or modification to existing ways of doing things. To offer suggestions to overcome obstacles—actual or anticipated—that may impede progress.

Procedure:

1. The facilitator gives each participant two index cards. (5 minutes)

On the first index card, participants silently write two hopes they have for the work being considered or work that is under way. A question-prompt for writing Hopes is this: *If this new idea/endeavor works as planned, what are the likely benefits of doing it?*

On the second index card, they write two fears they have associated with the work. A question-prompt for writing Fears is this: *If this new idea/endeavor doesn't go or isn't going as planned, what are the dangers or obstacles that may result or are present?*

2. The facilitator collects the cards, shuffles them, and redistributes the Hopes cards back to the group.

3. Without divulging the author, each participant reads aloud the Hope on the index card he has been given. These are shared without discussion. (5 minutes)

4. Without divulging the authors, the facilitator reads aloud the Fears index cards and invites a brief discussion (3–4 minutes) after each. The goal of the discussion is to promote a deeper understanding of the fears, provide solutions where appropriate (though this is not necessary for each card), and suggest things that might be done to alleviate or avoid the circumstances that are fearful. (45 minutes)

5. The process is debriefed and any unattended fears are placed in the *Parking Lot** for future consideration as the group moves forward with the work. (5 minutes)

---

*The *Parking Lot* is a piece of chart paper generally posted in the PLC meeting room on which participants write issues or concerns that have not been fully addressed or resolved but can be temporarily "parked" so that the group can continue to move forward. (I have participants write concerns on sticky notes and place those on the *Parking Lot* chart paper so that the notes can be removed when the concerns are later resolved.)

Inquiring Introductions Protocol

An activity to sharpen the listening and
questioning skills of members in a PLC.
Developed by Anne E. Jones.

Time: 35–45 minutes (depending on group size)

Procedure:

1. Participants form groups of four to six people.

2. Each participant quietly writes on an index card his responses to the following:
   a. Full name
   b. Subject and/or grade level taught (or title, if the participant is in a support position)
   c. One vacation experience you have had or plan to have (one or two sentences)

3. Rounds.

Each round begins with one member of the group being designated the *Introducer*, who shares the information on her card. After the Introducer makes her introduction by sharing her card, another participant asks a question of the Introducer, who answers the question in a sentence or two (no more than a brief paragraph).

When she finishes answering the question, a second participant will ask the Introducer a follow-up question. The Introducer answers this question with a brief response. After she does this, a third participant asks a new follow-up question based on the response heard. The Introducer will respond and the next participant asks a follow-up question and so on until all members have asked a single question of the Introducer, who responds to each.

The Catch: Each question that is asked must be *directly related* to the most recent statement made by the Introducer, namely, the last statement she made in response to the previous participant's question.

Each member of the group takes a turn being the Introducer, with each of the other participants asking a question in turn.

Examining Assessments

Developed by Gene Thompson-Grove.

Getting Started:

- The facilitator reminds the group of its norms and establishes time limits for each part of the process.

- The designated person in the group gives a brief description of the assessment's purpose and context, and answers a few clarifying questions, if necessary.

Describing the Assessment:

- The facilitator asks: "What do you see?"

- During this period the group gathers as much information as possible from the Assessment. Group members describe what they see, avoiding judgments about the quality of the assessment or interpretations about what the assessment asks students to do. If judgments or interpretations do arise, the facilitator should ask the person to describe the evidence on which they are based. It may be useful to list the group's observations on chart paper. If interpretations come up, they can be listed in another column for later discussion.

Completing the Assessment:

- Group members complete (parts of) the assessment.

Interpreting the Assessment:

- The facilitator asks: "From the students' perspective, what are they working on as they complete this assessment?"

- The facilitator then asks: "If this assessment was completed successfully by a student, what would it tell us about what this student knows, understands, and is able to do?"

- During this period, the group tries to make sense of what the assessment asks students to do. The group should try to find as many different interpretations as possible and evaluate them against the kind and quality of evidence in the previous steps. As you listen to each other's interpretations, ask questions that help you better understand each other's perspectives.

Implications for Our Practice:

- The facilitator asks: "What are the implications of this work for teaching, learning and assessment?"

• Based on the group's observations and interpretations, discuss any implications this—and the conversation thus far—might have for teaching, student learning, and assessment in the school. What teaching and learning issues have been raised for you in terms of your own practice? What issues have been raised in terms of schoolwide practices?

Reflecting on the Process:

• As a group, share what you have learned.

• Reflect on how well the process worked—what went well, and what could be improved.

Peeling the Onion: Developing a Problem Protocol

Developed in the field by educators affiliated with NSRF.

Purpose: To provide a structured way to develop an appreciation for the complexity of a problem in order to avoid the inclination to start out by "solving" the problem before it has been fully defined.

Procedure: As with all protocols, it is important to identify a facilitator who is responsible for keeping the group to the allotted time. This allows the group to maintain focus and keep on track, and frees the group to do its best thinking. The facilitator reviews the process with the group and then it begins. The times for each step can be adjusted to fit the available amount of time and the number of people in the group.

Facilitation Tips: Most of us are eager to solve problems before we truly understand their depth. This protocol is designed to help us peel away the layers in order to address the deeper issues that lie underneath the surface. If the problem were easy to solve, it would not still be a concern to the group. The facilitator should keep to the times strictly and gently remind people when they are giving advice too early.

The Protocol:

1. The keepers of the problem describe the problem/dilemma and ask a question to help focus the group's responses. (5 minutes)

2. Clarifying questions from group members to the presenters (these must be purely informational). (3 minutes)

3. A round where everyone says: "What I heard [the presenters say] is . . ." (The presenters are silent and take notes.)

4. A round where everyone says: "One assumption that seems to be part of the problem/dilemma is . . ." Or, "One thing I assume to be true about this problem is . . ." (The presenters are silent and take notes.)

5. Another round where everyone says: "A question this raises for me is . . ." (The presenters are silent and take notes).

6. [Perhaps] another round where everyone says: "Further questions this raises for me are . . ." (The presenters are silent and take notes.)

7. Another round where everyone asks: "What if . . . ?" Or, "Have we thought about . . . ?" Or, "I wonder . . . ?" (The presenters are silent and take notes.)

8. Presenters review their notes and say, "Having heard these comments and questions, now I think . . ." (The group members are silent and take notes.)

9. Now what? Together, the presenter and consultants talk about the possibilities and options that have surfaced.

10. Debrief the process. How was this like peeling an onion? What about the process was useful? Frustrating?

Passion Profiles Activity

Adapted from Gene Thompson-Grove's "Student Profiles," by Pedro Bermudez, Delkis Cabrera, and Linda Emm.

Pas·sion 1. A powerful emotion, such as love, joy, hatred, or anger. 2. Ardent love. 3. Boundless enthusiasm.

Read the passion profiles and identify the passion that most accurately describes who you are as an educator. If several fit (this will be true for many of you), choose the one that affects you the most, or the one that seems most significant as you reflect on your practice over time. (5 minutes)

Without using the number of the passion profile, ask your colleagues questions and find the people who chose the same profile you did. (5 minutes)

Directions for Small Groups:

1. Choose a facilitator/timer and a recorder/reporter.

2. Check to see if you all really share that passion. Then, talk about your school experiences together. What is it like to have this passion—to be this kind of educator? Each person in the group should have an opportunity to talk, uninterrupted, for 2 minutes. (10 minutes)

3. Next, each person in the group privately identifies an actual student, by name, who has been affected by the group's profile. Write [in your journal]: (5 minutes)

- What have I done with this student?
- What's worked? What hasn't?
- What else could I do?
- What questions does this raise for me?

4. Talk as a group about the questions that teachers who share this passion are likely to have about their practice. List as many of these questions as you can. (15 minutes)

Recorder/reporter should write on the newsprint, and should be ready to report out succinctly to the large group. Be sure to put your passion profile # at the top of the newsprint page.

5. Whole group debrief (after hearing from each passion profile group): (15 minutes)

- What strikes you as you listen to the passions of these educators? Listen for the silences. Where are they, and what do you make of them?
- Which of the questions generated intrigues you the most? Why? How might you go about exploring this question with colleagues? What would you do first?

Passion Profiles

Adapted from Gene Thompson-Grove's "Student Profiles,"
by Pedro R. Bermudez, Belkis Cabrera, and Linda Emm.

Passion 1: The Child

You became a teacher primarily because you wanted to make a difference in the life of a child. Perhaps you were one of those kids whose life was changed by a committed, caring teacher and you decided to become a teacher so that you could do that for other children. You are always curious about particular students whose work and/or behavior just doesn't seem to be in sync with the rest of the students in your class. You often wonder about how peer interactions seem to affect a student's likelihood to complete assignments, or what enabled one of your ELL students to make such remarkable progress seemingly overnight, or how to motivate a particular student to get into the habit of writing. You believe that understanding the unique qualities that each student brings to your class is the key to unlocking their full potential as learners.

Passion 2: The Curriculum

You are one of those teachers who are always "tinkering" with the curriculum in order to enrich the learning opportunities for your students. You have a thorough understanding of your content area. You attend conferences and subscribe to journals that help you to stay up on current trends affecting the curriculum that you teach. Although you are often dissatisfied with "what is" with respect to the prescribed curriculum in your school or district, you are almost always sure that you could do it better than the frameworks. You are always critiquing the existing curriculum and finding ways to make it better for the kids you teach, especially when you have a strong hunch that "there is a better way to do this."

Passion 3: Content Knowledge

You are at your best in the classroom when you have a thorough understanding of the content and/or topic you are teaching. Having to teach something you don't know much about makes you uncomfortable and always motivates you to hone this area of your teaching knowledge base. You realize that what you know about what you are teaching will influence how you can get it across to your students in a developmentally appropriate way. You spend a considerable amount of your personal time—both during the school year and in the summer—looking for books, material, workshops, and courses you can take that will strengthen your content knowledge.

Passion 4: Teaching Strategies and Techniques

You are motivated most as a teacher by a desire to improve on and experiment with teaching strategies and techniques. You have experienced and understand the value of particular strategies to engage students in powerful learning and want to get really good at this stuff. Although you have become really comfortable with using cooperative learning with your students, there are many other strategies and techniques that interest you and that you want to incorporate into your teaching repertoire.

Passion 5: The Relationship Between Beliefs and Professional Practice

You sense a "disconnect" between what you believe and what actually happens in your classroom and/or school. For example, you believe that a major purpose of schools is to produce citizens capable of contributing to and sustaining a democratic society; however, students in your class seldom get an opportunity to discuss controversial issues because you fear that the students you teach may not be ready and/or capable of this and you are concerned about losing control of the class.

Passion 6: The Intersection Between Your Personal and Professional Identities

You came into teaching from a previous career and often sense that your previous professional identity may be in conflict with your new identity as an educator. You feel ineffective and frustrated when your students or colleagues don't approach a particular task that is second nature to you because of your previous identity—writer, actor, artist, researcher, etc.—in the same way that you do. What keeps you up at night is how to use the knowledge, skills, and experiences you bring from your previous life to make powerful teaching and learning happen in your classroom and/or school.

Passion 7: Advocating Equity and Social Justice

You became an educator to change the world—to help create a more just, equitable, democratic, and peaceful planet. You are constantly thinking of ways to integrate issues of race, class, disability, power, etc. into your teaching; however, your global concerns for equity and social justice sometimes get in the way of your effectiveness as an educator—like the parent backlash that resulted from the time you showed *Schindler's List* to your sixth grade class. You know there are more developmentally appropriate ways to infuse difficult and complex issues into your teaching and want to learn more about how to do this with your students.

Passion 8: Context Matters

What keeps you up at night is how to keep students focused on learning despite the many disruptions that go on in your classroom/building on a daily basis. It seems that the school context conspires against everything that you know about teaching and learning—adults who don't model the behaviors they want to see reflected in the students, policies that are in conflict with the school's mission, and above all, a high stakes testing environment that tends to restrain the kind of teaching and learning that you know really works for the students you teach.

References and Further Reading

Anderson, L. W., & Krathwohl, D. R. (2001). *A taxonomy for learning, teaching, and assessing: A revision of Bloom's taxonomy of educational objectives.* New York: Longman.

Ainsworth, L., & Viegut, D. (2006). *Common formative assessments: An essential part of the integrated whole.* Thousand Oaks, CA: Corwin.

Baccellieri, P. (2009). *Professional learning communities.* Huntington Beach, CA: Shell Education.

Bolman, L., & Deal, T. (1994). *Becoming a teacher leader.* Thousand Oaks, CA: Corwin.

Boudett, K., City, E., & Murnane, R. (2005). *Data wise: A step-by-step guide to using assessment results to improve teaching and learning.* Cambridge, MA: Harvard Education Publishing Group.

Boudett, K., & Steele, J. (2007). *Data wise in action: Stories of schools using data to improve teaching and learning.* Cambridge, MA: Harvard Education Press.

Brophy, J., & Good, T. (2002). *Looking in classrooms* (9th ed.). Boston: Allyn & Bacon.

Buffum, A., Mattos, M., & Weber, C. (2008). *Pyramid response to intervention.* Bloomington, IN: Solution Tree.

Buffum, A., Mattos, M., & Weber, C. (2009). *Pyramid response to intervention: RTI, professional learning communities, and how to respond when kids don't learn.* Bloomington, IN: Solution Tree.

Burnette, R., DuFour, R., & Eaker, R. (2002). *Getting started: Reculturing schools to become professional learning communities.* Bloomington, IN: Solution Tree.

Chappuis, S., Chappuis, J., & Stiggins, R. (2009, February). Supporting teacher learning teams. *Educational Leadership, 66*(5), 56–60.

Collins, J. (2001). *Good to great: Why some companies make the leap . . . and others don't.* New York: Harper Business.

Costa, A., & Garmston, R. (1994). *Cognitive coaching.* Norwood, MA: Christopher-Gordon Publishers.

Covey, S. (1989). *The seven habits of highly effective people: Powerful lessons in personal change.* New York: Fireside.

Crane, T., & Patrick, L. (2007). *The heart of coaching.* San Diego, CA: FTA Press.

Darling-Hammond, L., & Richardson, N. (2009, February). Teacher learning: What matters? *Educational Leadership, 66*(5), 46–53.

David, J. (2009, October). Learning communities for administrators. *Educational Leadership, 67*(2), 88–89.

Deal, T., & Peterson, K. (1990). *The principal's role in shaping school culture.* Washington, DC: United States Department of Education.

Deal, T., & Peterson, K. (1999). *Shaping school culture: The heart of leadership.* San Francisco: Jossey-Bass.

DuFour, R. (2008, December). *PLCs at work: Bring the big ideas to life.* Paper presented at Charlotte-Mecklenburg Schools, Charlotte, NC.

DuFour, R., DuFour, R., & Eaker, R. (2008). *Revisiting professional learning communities at work™: New insights for improving schools.* Bloomington, IN: Solution Tree.

DuFour, R., DuFour, R., Eaker, R., & Karhanek, G. (2004). *Whatever it takes: How a professional learning community responds when kids don't learn.* Bloomington, IN: Solution Tree.

DuFour, R., DuFour, R., Eaker, R., & Many, T. (2006). *Learning by doing: A handbook for professional learning communities at work™.* Bloomington, IN: Solution Tree.

DuFour, R., & Eaker, R. (1998). *Professional learning communities at work: Best practices for enhancing student achievement.* Bloomington, IN: Solution Tree.

DuFour, R., Eaker, R., & DuFour, R. (2005). *On common ground: The power of professional learning communities.* Bloomington, IN: Solution Tree.

Dylan, B. (2004). *Lyrics: 1962–2001.* New York: Simon & Schuster.

Eason-Watkins, B., DuFour, R., Fullan, M., Eaker, R., DuFour, R., & Lezotte, L. (2005). *On common ground.* Bloomington, IN: Solution Tree.

Evans, R. (2001). *The human side of school change: Reform, resistance, and the real-life problems of innovation.* San Francisco: Jossey-Bass.

Francis, D., & Young, D. (1992). *Improving work groups: A practical manual for team building.* Washington, DC: Pfeiffer.

Friedman, T. L. (2007). *The world is flat: A brief history of the twenty-first century.* New York: Picador.

Fullan, M. (1993). *Change forces.* London: Falmer Press.

Fullan, M. (2001). *Leading in a culture of change.* San Francisco: Jossey-Bass.

Fullan, M. (2009, October). Leadership development: The larger context. *Educational Leadership, 67*(2), 45–49.

Gardner, H. (2004). *Changing minds: The art and science of changing our own and other people's minds.* Boston: Harvard Business School.

Gregory, G. H., & Kuzmich, L. (2004). *Data driven differentiation in the standards-based classroom.* Thousand Oaks, CA: Corwin.

Hall, G., & Hord, S. (1987). *Change in schools: Facilitating the process.* Albany, NY: SUNY Press.

Hargreaves, A., & Fink, D. (2006). *Sustainable leadership.* San Francisco: Wiley.

Hord, S., Rutherford, W., Huling-Austin, L., & Hall, G. (1987). *Taking charge of change.* Alexandria, VA: Association for Supervision and Curriculum Development.

Hord, S., & Sommers, W. (2008). *Leading professional learning communities.* Thousand Oaks, CA: Corwin.

Joyce, B., & Showers, B. (1995). *Student achievement through staff development: Fundamentals of school renewal* (2nd ed.). White Plains, NY: Longman.

Kanold, T. (2006). The continuous improvement wheel of a professional learning community *Journal of Staff Development, 27*(2), 16–21.

Katzenbach, J., & Smith, D. (1993). *The wisdom of teams: Creating the high-performance organization.* Boston: Harvard Business School.

Kendall, J., & Marzano, R. (2000). *Content knowledge: A compendium of standards and benchmarks for K–12 education* (3rd ed.). Alexandria, VA: Association for Supervision and Curriculum Development.

Kise, J. A. (2006). *Differentiated coaching: A framework for helping teachers change.* Thousand Oaks, CA: Corwin.

Kohm, B., & Nance, B. (2009, October). Creating collaborative cultures. *Educational Leadership, 67*(2), 67–72.

Kotter, J. (1996). *Leading change.* Boston: Harvard Business School.

Lencioni, P. (2002). *The five dysfunctions of a team: A leadership fable.* San Francisco: Jossey-Bass.

Lencioni, P. (2005). *Overcoming the five dysfunctions of a team: A field guide.* San Francisco: Jossey-Bass.

Lipton, L., & Wellman, B. (2007, September). How to talk so teachers listen. *Educational Leadership, 65*(1), 30–34.

Marzano, R. (1992). *A different kind of classroom: Teaching with dimensions of learning.* Alexandria, VA: Association for Supervision and Curriculum Development.

Marzano, R. (2003). *What works in schools: Translating research into action.* Alexandria, VA: Association for Supervision and Curriculum Development.

Marzano, R. (2007, March). *Classroom assessment and grading in a standards-based system.* Paper presented at the ASCD annual conference, Anaheim, CA.

Marzano, R., Pickering, D., & McTighe, J. (1993). Assessing student outcomes. Alexandria, VA: Association for Supervision and Curriculum Development.

Marzano, R., Waters, T., & McNulty, B. (2005). *School leadership that works.* Alexandria, VA: Association for Supervision and Curriculum Development.

McDonald, J. P., Mohr, N., Dichter, A., & McDonald, E. C. (2007). *The power of protocols: An educator's guide to better practice.* New York: Teachers College Press.

McEwan, E. K. (2005). *How to deal with teachers who are angry, troubled, exhausted, or just plain confused.* Thousand Oaks, CA: Corwin.

McTighe, J., & Wiggins, G. (2004). *Understanding by design: Professional development workbook.* Alexandria, VA: Association for Supervision and Curriculum Development.

NASDSE (2006). *Response to intervention.* A joint paper presented by the National Association of State Directors of Special Education and the Council of Administrators of Special Education at the Council for Exceptional Children. Retrieved from http://www.nasdse.org/Portals/0/Documents/Download%20Publications/RtIAnAdministratorsPerspective1–06.pdf

National Assessment of Educational Progress (NAEP). (2009a). *The nation's report card: Mathematics 2009* (National Center for Education Statistics No. 2010451). Retrieved from http://nces.ed.gov/pubsearch/pubsinfo.asp?pubid=2010451

National Assessment of Educational Progress (NAEP). (2009b). *The nation's report card: Reading 2009* (National Center for Education Statistics No. 2010458). Retrieved from http://nces.ed.gov/pubsearch/pubsinfo.asp?pubid=2010458

Nave, B. (2000). *Among critical friends: A study of critical friends groups in three Maine schools.* Doctoral dissertation, Harvard University, Cambridge, MA (Publication No. AAT 9968318). Retrieved from ProQuest Digital Dissertations database.

Newmann, F., & Wehlage, G. (1995). *Successful school restructuring: A report to the public and educators by the Center on Organization and Restructuring of Schools.* Madison: University of Wisconsin.

Newmann, F., & Wehlage, G. (1996). Restructuring for authentic student achievement. In F. Newmann (Ed.), *Authentic achievement: Restructuring schools for intellectual quality* (pp. 286–301). San Francisco: Jossey-Bass.

Palmer, P. J. (2007). *The courage to teach: Exploring the inner landscape of a teacher's life* (10th ed.). San Francisco: Jossey-Bass.

Patterson, K., Grenny, J., McMillan, R., & Switzler, A. (2002). *Crucial conversations: Tools for talking when stakes are high.* New York: McGraw-Hill.

Pfeffer, J., & Sutton, R. (2000). *The knowing-doing gap: How smart companies turn knowledge into action.* Boston: Harvard Business School.

Popham, W. (2008). *Transformative assessment.* Alexandria, VA: ASCD.

Ravitch, D. (2010). *The death and life of the great American school system.* New York: Basic Books.

Reason, C., & Reason, L. (2007, September). Asking the right questions. *Educational Leadership, 65*(1), 36–40.

Reeves, D. (2000). *Accountability in action: A blueprint for learning organizations.* Denver, CO: Advanced Learning.

Reeves, D. (2004). *Accountability for learning: How teachers and school leaders can take charge.* Alexandria, VA: Association for Supervision and Curriculum Development.

Reeves, D. (2005). *On common ground: The power of professional learning communities.* Bloomington, IN: Solution Tree.

Reeves, D. (2006). *The learning leader.* Alexandria, VA: Association for Supervision and Curriculum Development.

Reeves, D. (2008, February). Effective grading practices. *Educational Leadership, 65*(5), 85–87.

Reeves, D. B. (2009). *Leading change in your school.* Alexandria, VA: Association for Supervision and Curriculum Development.

Reeves, D. B. (2010). *Transforming professional development into student results.* Alexandria, VA: ASCD.

Rogers, S. (2009). *Teaching for excellence.* Evergreen, CO: PEAK Learning Systems.

Rooney, J. (2009, September). The craft of conversation. *Educational Leadership, 67*(1), 87–88.

Schmoker, M. (2003). First things first: Demystifying data analysis. Educational Leadership, 60(5), 22–24.

Schmoker, M. (2006). *Results now.* Alexandria, VA: Association for Supervision and Curriculum Development.

Scriffiny, P. (2008, October). Seven reasons for standards-based grading. *Educational Leadership, 66*(2), 70–74.

Semadeni, J. (2009). *Taking charge of professional development.* Alexandria, VA: Association for Supervision and Curriculum Development.

Semadeni, J. (2010, May). When teachers drive their learning. *Educational Leadership, 67*(8), 66–69.

Senge, P. (1990). *The fifth discipline: The art & practice of the learning organization.* New York: Doubleday/Currency.

Senge, P., Kleiner, A., Roberts, C., Ross, R., & Smith, B. (1994). *The fifth discipline fieldbook: Strategies and tools for building a learning organization.* New York: Doubleday/Currency.

Sergiovanni, T. (1994). *Building community in schools.* San Francisco: Jossey-Bass.

Sizer, T. R. (1984). *Horace's compromise: The dilemma of the American high school.* Boston: Houghton Mifflin.

Stiggins, R. (2001). *Student-involved classroom assessment* (3rd ed.). Upper Saddle River, NJ: Prentice Hall.

Stiggins, R. (2002). Assessment crisis: The absence of assessment for learning. *Phi Delta Kappan, 83*(10), 758–765.

Stiggins, R. (2004). New assessment beliefs for a new school mission. *Phi Delta Kappan, 86*(1), 22–27.

Stiggins, R. J., Arter, J. A., Chappuis, J., & Chappius, S. (2010). *Classroom assessment for student learning: Doing it right—using it well.* Boston: Allyn & Bacon.

Straus, D. (2002). *How to make collaboration work: Powerful ways to build consensus, solve problems, and make decisions.* San Francisco: Berrett-Koehler.

Trends in International Mathematics and Science Study (TIMSS). (2007). *Highlights from TIMSS 2007: Mathematics and science achievement of U.S. fourth- and eighth-grade students in an international context* (National Center for Education Statistics No. 2009001). Retrieved from http://nces.ed.gov/pubsearch/pubsinfo.asp?pubid=2009001

Tomlinson, C. A. (2001). *How to differentiate instruction in mixed ability classrooms* (2nd ed.). Alexandria, VA: Association for Supervision and Curriculum Development.

U.S. Department of Education, National Center for Education Statistics. (2008). *Beginning teacher longitudinal study.* Retrieved from http://nces.ed.gov/surveys/btls/waves.asp

Whitaker, T. (2004). *What great teachers do differently.* Larchmont, NY: Eye On Education, Inc.

Wiggins, G., & McTighe, J. (2004). *Understanding by design.* Alexandria, VA: ASCD.

Wolfe, P. (2001). *Brain matters: Translating research into classroom practice.* Alexandria, VA: ASCD.

INTERNET SITES

All Things PLC: http://www.allthingsplc.info

Annenberg Institute of School Reform: http://www.annenberginstitute.org

ASCD (formerly Association for Supervision and Curriculum Development): http://www.ascd.org

Authentic Education: http://www.grantwiggins.org

Center for Authentic PLCs: http://www.authenticplcs.com

Center for Performance Assessment: http://www.makingstandards work.com

Coalition of Essential Schools: http://www.essentialschools.org

National Center on Response to Intervention: http://www.rti4success.org

National School Reform Faculty: http://www.nsrfharmony.org

National Staff Development Council: http://www.nsdc.org

School Reform Initiative: http://schoolreforminitiative.org

The Leadership and Learning Center: http://www.leadandlearn.com

Index